Scott Foresman

Reading

Grade 3

Phonics
Take-Home
Readers

Scott Foresman
Phonics System

Scott Foresman

Editorial Offices: Glenview, Illinois • New York, New York

Sales Offices: Reading, Massachusetts • Duluth, Georgia • Glenview, Illinois
Carrollton, Texas • Menlo Park, California

Editorial Offices
Glenview, Illinois • New York, New York

Sales Offices
Reading, Massachusetts • Duluth, Georgia • Glenview, Illinois
Carrollton, Texas • Menlo Park, California

ISBN 0-673-61260-0

9 10-CRK-06 05 04 03

TABLE OF CONTENTS

Phonics Readers for Unit 1

Book 1 Dick Whittington and His Cat
Short vowels

Book 2 Muffin Mix-Up
Double consonants (medial and final)

Book 3 The Sea
Long e digraphs; Long e spelled y and e

Book 4 Hooray for Tay-Tay!
Long a digraphs; Long o digraphs; Long o spelled o

Book 5 Night Animals
Long i spelled igh and y; Long u spelled u_e; Long u spelled u

Phonics Readers for Unit 2

Book 6 The Rainforest: What Is It Like?
Compound words

Book 7 Miss Loon's Missing Spoon
Vowel digraph oo

Book 8 The Hound on South Road
Vowel digraph ou; Vowel diphthong ou

Book 9 The Jade Gerbil
Consonants j and g/j/; Consonants s and c/s/

Book 10 Growing Up in Colonial Times
Vowel digraph ow; Vowel diphthong ow

Phonics Readers for Unit 3

Book 11 The Wrong Hat
Silent letters wr, kn, st, gn, mb

Book 12 Proud to Be a Farm Girl
R-controlled vowels

Book 13 Amazing Buildings
Base words

Book 14 The Really Lucky Dog
Suffixes -ness, -ly, -ful, -ous

Book 15 Truthful Juan
Medial consonant digraphs: th, ph, sh, ch

Phonics Readers for Unit 4

Book 16 Animal Tracks
Initial and final consonant blends

Book 17 The Splash on Spring Street
Three-letter blends

Book 18 Cowboys on the Trail
Vowel diphthongs oi, oy

Book 19 My New Friend's Noodles
Possessives (singular and plural)

Book 20 Why Mosquitoes Buzz in People's Ears
R-controlled vowels

...ders for Unit 5

...k 22 A Tale of Two Slugs
Plurals (regular and irregular)

Book 22 Earthquakes: What Causes
Them?
Consonant /k/ spelled c, ck, ch

Book 23 The Case of the Impolite
Poodle
Prefixes im-, dis-, non-

Book 24 Polar Bears: Living in the
Arctic
Inflected endings

Book 25 The Whiz Kid and the
Whopper
Consonant digraph wh;
Consonant /h/ spelled wh

Phonics Readers for Unit 6

Book 26 The Story of Helen Keller
Schwa sound

Book 27 The Brave Little Tailor
Syllabication; Common syllable
patterns for word identification

Book 28 All Because Maud and Tom
Were Bored
Vowel digraphs aw, au, /ȯ/
spelled al

Book 29 Inventions, Old and New
Vowel digraphs ui, ew

Book 30 Penny's Unusually Good Day
Affixes

Scott Foresman
Reading

Grade 3
Phonics Reader 1

**Dick Whittington
and His Cat**
retold by Lee S. Justice
illustrated by
Gregory Nemec

Phonics Skill:
• Short vowels

Scott Foresman
Phonics System

Scott Foresman

Dick Whittington and His Cat

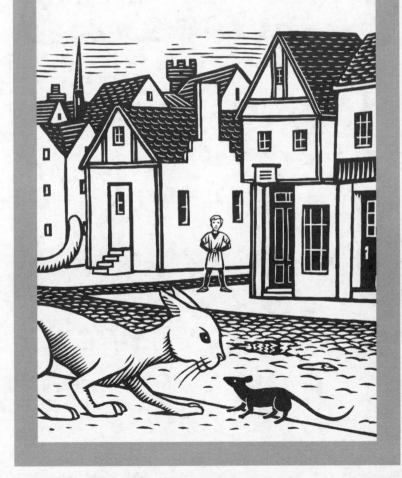

retold by Lee S. Justice
illustrated by Gregory Nemec

This book belongs to

_____

Phonics for Families: This book gives your child practice in reading words with the short vowel sounds. After your child reads the book aloud to you, ask him or her to point out words with the short vowel sounds.

Phonics Skill: Short vowels

Scott Foresman
Reading

Grade 3
Phonics Reader 2

Muffin Mix-Up
by Susan Blackaby
illustrated by
Len Ebert

Phonics Skill:
• Double consonants
(medial and final)

Scott Foresman
Phonics
System

Scott Foresman

by Susan Blackaby
illustrated by Len Ebert

This book belongs to

_____

Phonics for Families: This book gives your child practice reading words with double consonants, such as *muffins* and *still*. After reading the story, work together to write words with double consonants, using the story words and objects in the illustrations.

Phonics Skill: Double consonants (medial and final)

Anna and Carlos ate the muffins—along with some milk. Everything was excellent!

When dinner was over, Carlos said, "Let's do this again tomorrow."

"Okay," said Anna, "but next time you just stay here and wait for me. Hmm, maybe we'll make carrot muffins tomorrow."

16

Muffin Mix-Up

by Susan Blackaby
illustrated by Len Ebert

Scott Foresman

Editorial Offices: Glenview, Illinois • New York, New York
Sales Offices: Reading, Massachusetts • Duluth, Georgia
Glenview, Illinois • Carrollton, Texas • Menlo Park, California

It was a sunny summer day. Anna liked her buddy, Carlos. So, she thought she would surprise him with a little present. "Carlos will love this," thought Anna.

They went to Mr. Vetter's store and got everything they needed. Then they hurried home to make the muffins.

When the muffins were ready, it was time for dinner.

"Pretty funny, buddy," giggled Carlos.

"I'll say," said Anna. "But now we're both here. So let's go make those muffins."

"Great," said Carlos. "But first we should go shopping. We need other things to make the muffins, like vanilla and butter."

Anna skipped over to Carlos's house. She rang the bell. No one answered.

"Carlos!" Anna called.

There was still no answer.

"That's funny," thought Anna. "I wonder where Carlos is."

Anna sat down on the step. Then Carlos's puppy, Pepper, trotted along.

"Hi, Pepper!" said Anna. "Do you know where Carlos is?"

Pepper just looked at Anna. Then, he suddenly jumped up.

© Scott Foresman 3

"Why did you come to my house?" asked Carlos.

"I came to bring you a muffin tin so that we can make blueberry muffins!" said Anna. Then she handed the muffin tin to Carlos.

"Why did you go to my house?" asked
Anna.

"I wanted to give you these blueberries
so that we can make blueberry muffins,"
said Carlos.

Then he handed the bowl of berries
to Anna.

Pepper got mud all over Anna's dress.

"Gross!" said Anna, as she hopped to
her feet.

"You are no help!" said Anna.

Meanwhile, Carlos had gone to Anna's
house. He had a little surprise for her too!
"Anna will love this," thought Carlos.
Carlos skipped up to Anna's door.

Anna was still sitting on Carlos's porch.
"Where have you been?" asked Anna.
"I was at your house," said Carlos.
"We must have just missed each other,"
said Anna.
"I suppose we did," said Carlos.

© Scott Foresman 3

Carlos left Anna a message. Then he walked home.

He lifted the brass knocker and let it fall. Rap! Rap! Rap! No one answered.

"Anna!" called Carlos.

There was still no answer.

"That's odd," thought Carlos. "I wonder where Anna is."

As Carlos stood there, Anna's fuzzy kittens rubbed against him.

"Hi, kittens," said Carlos. "Do you know where Anna is?"

The kittens just played with the laces on Carlos's yellow sneakers.

One kitten fussed with the ribbon around her neck. The other kitten scratched her collar. "You are no help!" said Carlos.

© Scott Foresman 3

Scott Foresman
Reading

Grade 3
Phonics Reader 3

The Sea
by Anastasia Suen

Phonics Skills:
• Long *e* digraphs
• Long *e* spelled *y* and *e*

Scott Foresman
Phonics System

Scott Foresman

The Sea

by Anastasia Suen

This book belongs to

_____

Phonics for Families: This book features words with the long e sound. Invite your child to read the book aloud. Then have him or her find words with this sound in the story.

Phonics Skills: Long e digraphs; Long e spelled y and e

The ocean is filled with many beautiful and different animals. Each day as the Earth spins and the moon moves, the tides rise and fall. Waves wash onto the shore again and again, bringing us reminders of this wonderful place!

The Sea

by Anastasia Suen

Scott Foresman

Editorial Offices: Glenview, Illinois • New York, New York
Sales Offices: Reading, Massachusetts • Duluth, Georgia
Glenview, Illinois • Carrollton, Texas • Menlo Park, California

16

Most of the earth is covered with water, and most of that water is in the ocean. Many plants and animals live in the salty ocean water. Others live where the ocean touches the land, at the seashore.

These tube worms live on the ocean floor near deep-sea hot springs. These hot springs are also called deep-sea vents. The tube worms feed off the air and gas coming out of the vents. Deep-sea vents were discovered only recently. They are so deep that only a submarine can reach them.

Far out at sea, the ocean floor is very deep. It is so deep that no light shines there at all. Some animals that live near the ocean floor glow in the dark. An angler fish, which makes its home deep in the ocean, has a fin on top of its head that glows.

At the seashore, the water is always moving. Gravity from the moon pulls the water, causing the water level to rise and fall. This rising and falling of the water is called a tide. High tide brings the water far up onto the shore. Low tide leaves the beach dry and wide. Wind makes the waves roll in and out.

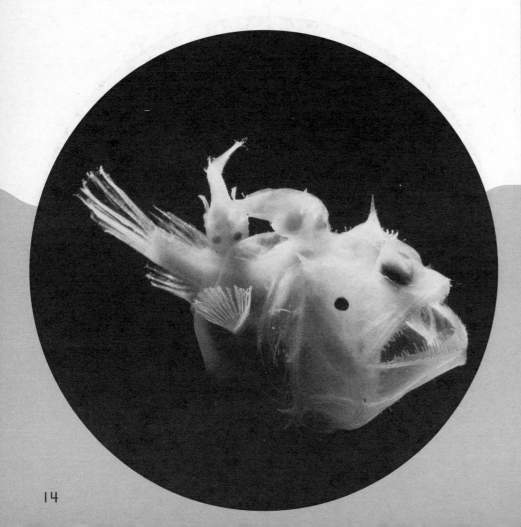

Some beaches are sandy and some are rocky. On a sandy beach, you can often see how high the tide came in. A line of dead seaweed is often left on the sand at the highest point. Below this line of seaweed, the beach might look empty, but it is not.

Rays, which are related to sharks, look like underwater birds when they swim. An octopus, which has no backbone, can squeeze between rocks in the ocean.

So many different animals live in the ocean. Sea turtles, which make their home in the ocean, have hard shells and can swim up to twenty miles an hour. Jellyfish, which also live in the ocean, have no bones and simply float from place to place.

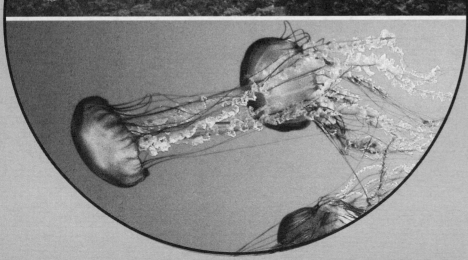

After a wave rolls out, these sandpipers run over and poke their bills into the sand. They are looking for something to eat. The bubbles in the sand might be telling you that something is hiding below.

On rocky beaches, the animals are easier to see. When the tide is low, you can see mussels, sea stars, and limpets clinging to the rocks. The rocks are covered with seaweed.

Fish that live in warm water are often very colorful. More types of fish live in the coral reefs than any other place in the ocean. Butterfly fish, clownfish, and parrotfish swim among the coral. Some sea stars and crabs live in the reefs too.

With a snorkel and mask, you can explore a coral reef. Most coral only grows in warm, clear, and shallow water because it needs light to stay alive. If you look closely at a piece of coral, you will see that it is soft on the inside and hard on the outside.

When the tide is high, the seaweed floats, and the sea stars and sea urchins move about. Mussels and limpets poke out of their shells. Crabs come out of their hiding places in the rocks and snails climb on the seaweed.

From a dock, you might see otters floating in the water and sea lions sunning themselves on the rocks. Sea otters like to float on their backs in the sea where seaweed grows.

When you climb aboard a whale-watching boat, you leave the shore behind. Pelicans and sea gulls often fly overhead. Sometimes dolphins follow your boat, splashing in the spray. And hopefully you see whales!

Scott Foresman
Reading

Grade 3
Phonics Reader 4

Hooray for Tay-Tay!
by Lucy Floyd
illustrated by
Elizabeth Wolf

Phonics Skills:
• Long *a* digraphs
• Long *o* digraphs
• Long *o* spelled *o*

Scott Foresman
Phonics System

Scott Foresman

Hooray for Tay-Tay!

by Lucy Floyd
illustrated by Elizabeth Wolf

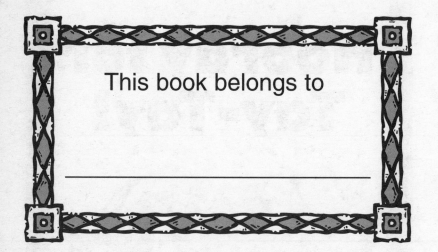

This book belongs to

_____

Phonics for Families: This book provides practice reading words with the long *a* and long *o* sounds, as in *bay, rain, goat,* and *gold*. Read the book aloud with your child. Then invite him or her to suggest a different ending for the story.

Phonics Skills: Long *a* digraphs; Long *o* digraphs; Long *o* spelled *o*

Tay-Tay did not win the prize for the
Most Unusual Pet. That prize went to the
skunk. However, the judges did give
Tay-Tay a prize for the Best Costume.

And everybody yelled, "Hooray for
Tay-Tay!"

16

Hooray for Tay-Tay!

by Lucy Floyd
illustrated by Elizabeth Wolf

Scott Foresman

Editorial Offices: Glenview, Illinois • New York, New York
Sales Offices: Reading, Massachusetts • Duluth, Georgia
Glenview, Illinois • Carrollton, Texas • Menlo Park, California

Ms. Fay bought a big house on a hill
that was covered with flowers. It was just
the home she had always wanted. She
could see sailboats floating in the bay.
And she could hear a train chugging
along behind her house.

Two judges were looking at the
animals and writing notes. When they
came to Tay-Tay, one judge said, "I'm not
sure what this is!"

Both judges stared at Tay-Tay's nose,
which was poking out from under the
hat. Then they wrote some notes.

Ms. Fay was trailing way behind her goat. But finally she came to the place where unusual pets were roaming around. She saw a toad, a skunk, and a poodle with a bad haircut. Then she saw Tay-Tay, walking around in the T-shirt and hat.

Ms. Fay liked to work around her new home. She patched holes on the porch, painted the steps, and planted roses. Folks living nearby were friendly, and they helped if Ms. Fay needed anything. They were happy to loan her a pail, a tray, a pole, or whatever she needed.

Ms. Fay was almost completely
happy. "But I need one more thing,"
she said to herself. "I need a pet.
I would take a dog, a cat, or whatever
comes along."

And one day, a stray did show up.

"I'm afraid to look," moaned Ms. Fay
as she ran after Tay-Tay. And sure
enough, Tay-Tay ran right into the hat
cart. Hats went flying everywhere. A
bright red one landed on Tay-Tay's head.

T-shirts went flying everywhere. A gold shirt landed on top of Tay-Tay. That did not stop him! Tay-Tay kept on trotting. And this time he headed straight for a cart that was loaded with hats.

"Not exactly what I had in mind," said Ms. Fay to the animal in her yard. "But okay. A goat will do." So the goat became her pet, and she named him Tay-Tay. Nobody ever knew why she called him this.

Tay-Tay had his own home in a shed in the yard. He liked to roam around the yard and nibble the grass. He also liked to nibble the roses. "Oh, well," said Ms. Fay, "there are enough roses for both of us. Nibble on, Tay-Tay."

"Tay-Tay," yelled Ms. Fay. "Look where you're going!"

But Tay-Tay trotted on and he ran right into the T-shirt cart.

"Oh, no!" groaned Ms. Fay.

"Oh, no!" cried Ms. Fay. "Come back here, Tay-Tay!" But Tay-Tay didn't listen at all. He headed straight for a cart that was loaded with T-shirts.

One day Ms. Fay woke up and it was raining. So she stayed inside and read her mail. She saw this notice:

Come to the Plainville Fair!

Saturday, May 1

Most Unusual Pet Contest!

Bring your pet!

"That sounds like just the contest for Tay-Tay," said Ms. Fay. "We're going to the fair!"

On Saturday, May 1, Ms. Fay washed Tay-Tay with soap, brushed his coat, and sprayed him with perfume. "Some folks think goats smell bad," she told Tay-Tay, "and we don't want to take any chances. Now we're ready for the Plainville Fair!"

The day was nice and sunny as Ms. Fay and Tay-Tay walked down the road by the bay. When they were almost at the Plainville Fair, Tay-Tay began pulling on his rope. Before Ms. Fay knew it, he was trotting away, far ahead of her.

8

9

Scott Foresman
Reading

Grade 3
Phonics Reader 5

Night Animals
by Marc Gave

Phonics Skills:
- Long *i* spelled *igh* and *y*
- Long *u* spelled *u_e*
- Long *u* spelled *u*

Scott Foresman
Phonics System

Scott Foresman

Night Animals

by Marc Gave

This book belongs to

_____

Phonics for Families: This book features words with the long *i* and long *u* sounds. Read the book with your child. Then have your child name words in this book that have the long *i* and long *u* sounds.

Phonics Skills: Long *i* spelled *igh* and *y*; Long *u* spelled *u_e*; Long *u* spelled *u*

The next time you say good night, think of all the animals that are just getting up!

Night Animals

by Marc Gave

Scott Foresman

Editorial Offices: Glenview, Illinois • New York, New York
Sales Offices: Reading, Massachusetts • Duluth, Georgia
Glenview, Illinois • Carrollton, Texas • Menlo Park, California

It's a warm summer night. You lie in bed and try to fall asleep. You close your eyes tight. But try as you might, you cannot fall asleep. Why not?

It's not a bright light outside. It's not cars passing or music playing. It might be the chirping of crickets, the peeping of tree frogs, or the sounds of other animals.

In the grasslands of Africa, nights are busy too. Lions hunt best at night. Leopards also hunt at night. Hippos leave the water to eat big meals of grass to fill their huge stomachs.

On a hot day in the desert, many animals sleep in holes and under plants. Why? They try to stay cool during the day. Then they come out at night when the air gets cooler.

It might be bedtime for humans. But these animals, and many more, stay wake at night. For them it's the right time to move about and find food. Some of these night animals may surprise you.

Fireflies are also called lightning bugs. There are many different kinds. Have you ever seen them light up? This is how fireflies talk to one another. Their flashing light sends a coded message that only the same kind of firefly will answer. The flashing happens at night because it would be harder to see in the daylight.

But raccoons are not shy! They often move about in the same places where humans live and work. You may have heard a raccoon looking in your garbage can. It was just looking for something good to eat!

Porcupines, possums, and raccoons also wake up when you are sleeping. They, like other animals, use the time looking for something to eat.

Porcupines stuff themselves with berries. Sometimes a mother possum has to take her babies off her back to find food for the family. Most of the time, these animals move about in the dark where there are no humans.

Moths look like butterflies, but they fly mostly at night. You might see moths flying around a light outside. If you open your door, one of them might fly in and flutter around a lamp.

Down below the fliers are creepers and crawlers that hide in the soil or under leaves during the day. Slugs and earthworms have bodies that would dry up in the sun. They wait until night to come above ground.

On the ground, mice hunt at night for seeds, berries, and nuts. The touch of their whiskers helps them find their way.

Another high flier is the owl. From dusk until dawn, owls patrol the night sky. Their eyes work better than human eyes do in dim light. And their ears can pick up sounds you might miss.

Frogs and toads also have bodies that dry up with too much sun. So they spend their days in water or in damp hiding places. At night they come out to catch insects.

At night bats leave caves or dark places where they have been sleeping during the day. They fly high in the night sky.

Some bats like to eat fruit. These bats use their sharp senses of sight and smell to find food. Other bats like to eat insects. These bats do not have good sight. But they have a special way of hearing that helps them find food.

Grade 3
Phonics Reader 6

**The Rainforest:
What Is It Like?**
by Marilee Robin Burton
illustrated by
Geoff McCormick

Phonics Skill:
• Compound words

The Rainforest:
What Is It Like?

by Marilee Robin Burton
illustrated by Geoff McCormick

This book belongs to

_____

Phonics for Families: This book will give your child practice reading compound words. After reading the book together, take turns finding the compound words.

Phonics Skill: Compound words

Today people are discovering how important rainforests are. There is worldwide interest in protecting them. We can start to help by learning more about them!

The Rainforest: What Is It Like?

by Marilee Robin Burton
illustrated by Geoff McCormick

Scott Foresman

Editorial Offices: Glenview, Illinois • New York, New York
Sales Offices: Reading, Massachusetts • Duluth, Georgia
Glenview, Illinois • Carrollton, Texas • Menlo Park, California

Try to picture a place that is sunny, warm and wet every day of the year. A place where each day is filled with sunshine and cooled by rainfall! A place where evergreen trees tower two hundred feet high. Flowers bloom in all colors and animals are everywhere.

Asian Rainforest

Today rainforests are in danger. They are cut down for timber. They are burned to make farmland. Some animals who once lived there can no longer survive.

Life in the rainforest is important to the world outside too. From the forest we get food, wood, and medicine. Scientists are always looking to make discoveries that will help everyone.

Asian Rainforest

This place has more kinds of plants and animals than anywhere else on Earth. It is Earth's oldest woodland. It was growing before there were dinosaurs. This place is a rainforest.

Tropical rainforests grow near the equator. This is halfway between the North and South Poles. The yearlong moist, warm weather is ideal for plants. There is no cold wintertime. Fruit ripens all year. Trees and vines grow thick and fast. Trees are always green. Other kinds of rainforests are found in other parts of the world.

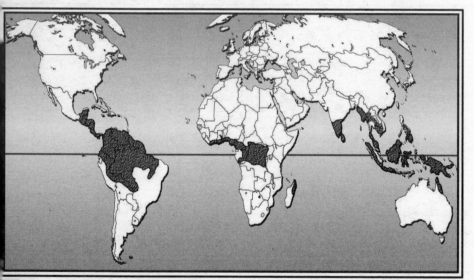

Tropical Rainforests

Plants and animals depend on each other. Dead plants enrich the soil. This soil is food for the living plants. Plants provide food for insects and some animals. Insects and small animals are food for larger creatures.

The plants and animals that live in the forest help each other. Many have special jobs. Monkeys, bats, and birds scatter seeds from mealtime fruits. Bees, bats, butterflies, and hummingbirds spread pollen that makes more flowers.

Animals make their homes everywhere. They live underground. They live in treetops. And they live in all the places in between. Look up, down, or sideways. Something will be creeping, crawling, or flying!

The woodlands are full of animals. Some, such as mice, ants, and parrots, you have seen before. Others are unusual. You probably have never seen a boa constrictor, a giant anteater, or a coati. They all make their homes in rainforests.

At the bottom is the forest floor. Large animals that cannot climb and thousands of tiny creatures live here. There is little sunlight. This does not seem to bother the animals. Leaf-cutter ants scurry along tiny highways carrying home food. Many different kinds of insects are all busy!

The canopy is so thick that not much sunlight reaches below it. The area underneath the canopy is dimly lit. This is called the understory. Little animals live in the smaller trees that grow here. Lizards roam. Butterflies flutter. Sleeping bats hang upside down and at mealtime jaguars prowl in this layer.

It is a crowded place! One hundred different kinds of trees can grow in a space the size of a football field. Fifty kinds of ants may crawl on the trunk of one evergreen. Nine hundred beetles may sleep in the fur of one sloth sleeping in that tree!

Tropical rainforests have different layers. Many animals live in the forest canopy. This is where the tall tree branches meet and often form a thick forest roof. It is a lush green platform. Frogs, birds, and monkeys enjoy living here.

Emergent

Canopy

Understory

Forest Floor

A few taller trees reach above the canopy. This uppermost level is the emergent layer. Eagles nest in these tall treetops. From there they peer down into the canopy.

Scott Foresman
Reading

Grade 3
Phonics Reader 7

Miss Loon's
Missing Spoon
by Nat Gabriel
illustrated by
Manuel King

Phonics Skill:
• Vowel digraph *oo*

Scott Foresman
Phonics
System

Scott Foresman

Miss Loon's Missing Spoon

by Nat Gabriel
illustrated by Manuel King

This book belongs to

_____

Phonics for Families: This book provides practice reading words in which the letters *oo* represent the sounds heard in *spoon* and *look*. After reading the book aloud, have your child find objects in the house whose names contain the sounds heard in *spoon* and *look*.

Phonics Skill: Vowel digraph *oo*

"I play the spoons!" said Miss Loon.

"If you had not found my missing spoon, I would not have been able to play."

"I'm glad I could help," said Mr. Hoot with a smile.

The band began to play. Mr. Hoot liked the horns and the drums, but best of all he liked the sound of Miss Loon's two spoons.

16

Miss Loon's Missing Spoon

by Nat Gabriel
illustrated by Manuel King

Scott Foresman

Editorial Offices: Glenview, Illinois • New York, New York
Sales Offices: Reading, Massachusetts • Duluth, Georgia
Glenview, Illinois • Carrollton, Texas • Menlo Park, California

"Hello, this is Miss Loon. I hear that you are very good at finding things. I am missing something very important. Do you think you can find it?"

© Scott Foresman 3

Mr. Hoot and Miss Loon floated away in the big balloon. They landed beside a school.

"What are we doing here?" asked Mr. Hoot.

"The band is playing tonight," said Miss Loon, "and I am in the band."

"What do you play?" asked Mr. Hoot.

"Good! You found my spoon just in time," said Miss Loon. "Come along now, we will take the balloon."

"The balloon? Where are we going?" asked Mr. Hoot.

"You will see soon," said Miss Loon.

"Yes, Miss Loon, this is Mr. Hoot. I am very good at finding things. What are you missing?"

"I've lost a very important spoon," said
Miss Loon.

"A spoon?" asked Mr. Hoot.

"Yes," said Miss Loon, "and I really need it!"

© Scott Foresman 3

Mr. Hoot found the boot. He looked
inside and there was the spoon! Mr. Hoot
came down the ladder with a proud smile on
his face.

"Miss Loon, I found your boot and your
spoon," he said proudly.

"Let's see. If I were a boot," said Mr. Hoot, "where would I be?"

"You might be on the roof," said Miss Loon.

"The roof?" asked Mr. Hoot. "Why would your boot be on the roof?"

"Because I put it there to stop the rain from coming in. Ah! Maybe I forgot to bring it down," said Miss Loon.

Mr. Hoot went up on the roof.

"Did you say you lost it?" asked Mr. Hoot.

"Well, I think maybe someone took it," cried Miss Loon.

"I'll be there soon!" said Mr. Hoot.

Then he ran to Miss Loon's house to see about the missing spoon.

"Tell me about the spoon, Miss Loon," said Mr. Hoot.

"It was in my room," she said. "It was inside my red boot."

"I see," said Mr. Hoot. "Why do you keep your spoon in your boot?"

"It's a very good place to keep it," said Miss Loon.

"I see," said Mr. Hoot, as he wrote some notes.

"Let's see. If I were a spoon," said Mr. Hoot, "where would I be?"

"You would be in my boot!" cried Miss Loon.

"Your boot is missing too!" said Mr. Hoot.

"Yes! Someone took my spoon and my boot," said Miss Loon.

"You must find my spoon soon!" cried
Miss Loon.

"I will," said Mr. Hoot.

Mr. Hoot looked all over for the missing
spoon. He found a broom but no spoon. He
found a book and a hook but no spoon.

"Miss Loon, did you use the spoon to eat
food?" asked Mr. Hoot.

"Never!" said Miss Loon.

"I see," said Mr. Hoot. "Did you wear the
boot on your foot?"

"Never!" said Miss Loon.

Mr. Hoot wrote some more notes.

"May I take a look in your room, Miss Loon?" asked Hoot.

Miss Loon took Hoot to her room. Hoot found a red boot with a big spoon inside it.

"Yes!" yelled Hoot. "Here is your spoon!"

Miss Loon shook her head. "That is not the missing spoon. That is my other spoon!"

"Do you have another boot too?" asked Mr. Hoot.

"Yes," said Miss Loon.

Mr. Hoot stopped to write some new notes.

© Scott Foresman 3

Scott Foresman
Reading

Grade 3
Phonics Reader 8

**The Hound on
South Road**
by Meish Goldish
illustrated by
Mordicai Gerstein

Phonics Skills:
• Vowel digraph *ou*
• Vowel diphthong *ou*

Scott Foresman
**Phonics
System**

Scott Foresman

The Hound on South Road

by Meish Goldish
illustrated by Mordicai Gerstein

This book belongs to

_____

Maria and her father left Rosa's house.
Rosa sat on the couch with her mother
and father.

"You know, I don't feel so bad," Rosa
said. "I really didn't lose a hound. I found
a new friend!"

16

The Hound on South Road

by Meish Goldish
illustrated by Mordicai Gerstein

Scott Foresman

Editorial Offices: Glenview, Illinois • New York, New York
Sales Offices: Reading, Massachusetts • Duluth, Georgia
Glenview, Illinois • Carrollton, Texas • Menlo Park, California

Rosa sat outside her house. None of her friends were around for the weekend. There was hardly a sound on South Road.

Just then, Rosa heard loud barking. She looked around. Sure enough, a dog was running up the road! Rosa could tell it was a hound.

Maria and her father were about to leave with their hound. But Rosa had something to say.

"Maria, would it be all right if I came to see you and Cloud sometime?" she asked.

"I would love that!" Maria shouted.

When Cloud saw Maria, he ran to her. Maria rubbed his snout. "Good dog," she said. "It's been so tough without you!"

Rosa could see how happy Cloud and Maria were together.

When the hound saw Rosa, he trotted over to her and licked his snout. Rosa knew that dogs did that so they could smell things better.

Rosa could see that the hound was friendly. He did not act rough. She touched his head and petted him. He did not have a tag to tell who he was.

© Scott Foresman 3

"Pretty hound!" Rosa said. The dog was brown with a big round spot of white. The round spot looked like a cloud.

"I should call you Cloud," Rosa said. "Yes, that is a good name for you. Cloud!"

"I'm Maria," the girl said. "This is my father. My cousin Carlos told us you found my hound."

"Yes," said Rosa. "I found him here on South Road."

"We live about nine miles from here," Maria's father said. "That hound really gets around!"

That night, Rosa fed Cloud some soup.
Then at six o'clock, the doorbell rang. Rosa
opened the door. Outside stood a young
girl and a tall man.

Rosa led Cloud inside the house to show
her mother and father.

"Look! I found a hound!" she shouted.
"May I keep it?"

Father called the dog pound. They
told him that no one had called about
a lost hound.

"Looks like you've got a dog," Father
said. "At least for now."

"Yes!" Rosa cried out loud.

All weekend, Rosa showed how well she could care for a dog. She played with Cloud. She would sit on the couch and bounce a ball. Cloud would pounce on the ball and bring it back in his mouth.

Rosa also made sure that Cloud had enough to eat. She even fed him soup!

"I know I shouldn't feel bad," cried Rosa. "But I do. I wish they wouldn't take Cloud away from me."

"I know," said Mother. "But if someone found something that belonged to you, wouldn't you want it back?"

"Yes, you're right," Rosa said, pouting a bit.

At home, Rosa told her mother what she had found out.

"I know all about it," Mother said. "Maria's father already called here. He and Maria are coming at around six o'clock to pick up their hound."

After each meal, Rosa went outside with Cloud. They would run around together in the playground.

On Monday afternoon, Rosa took Cloud
to the school playground. She wanted her
friends to see her hound.

A large group of children stood around
to touch Cloud. They liked to see him lick
his snout. "You are lucky!" they shouted.

But the next day, Rosa wasn't so lucky.
Carlos came up to her after school. He
said, "Rosa, I found out that your hound
really belongs to my cousin Maria. He ran
away from her farm last week."

Rosa's face turned pale. She was very
upset. Rosa felt grouchy all the way home.

Scott Foresman
Reading

Grade 3
Phonics Reader 9

The Jade Gerbil
by Jim Fremont
illustrated by
Patrick Merrell

Phonics Skills:
• Consonants *j* and *g*/j/
• Consonants *s* and *c*/s/

Scott Foresman
Phonics System

Scott Foresman

The Jade Gerbil

by Jim Fremont
illustrated by Patrick Merrell

This book belongs to

_____

Phonics for Families: This book features words with the *j*, soft *g*, *s*, and soft *c* sounds. Invite your child to read the book aloud and then work together to make up a new Jersey City Joe adventure.

Phonics Skill: Consonants *j* and *g/j/*;
Consonants *s* and *c/s/*

Joe's boss put the Jade Gerbil in a safe place.

"Good job!" Joe's boss said. "What are you going after next?"

Joe thought for about seven seconds. "I heard a legend about a lost city with gorgeous gems," Joe whispered.

"Can you leave right away?" asked Joe's boss.

16

The Jade Gerbil

by Jim Fremont
illustrated by Patrick Merrell

Scott Foresman

Editorial Offices: Glenview, Illinois • New York, New York
Sales Offices: Reading, Massachusetts • Duluth, Georgia
Glenview, Illinois • Carrollton, Texas • Menlo Park, California

Jersey City Joe worked for a man who collected expensive items. Joe read about a priceless piece called the Jade Gerbil.

"I'd like you to find the Jade Gerbil!" Joe's boss said. "Can you leave right away?"

Celia didn't notice Joe's clever trick until later. By then, Joe was safely on his way home.

But once Celia was out of sight, Joe checked his jacket. The Jade Gerbil was safe in his secret pocket.

"She'll soon see my pack is full of rocks," he said.

So Joe was off on another adventure. He filled his backpack with pajamas, pants, shirts, and socks. He added seeds and cereal. He jammed in maps and rope too. He tied skis on top. Then he put his jacket on and sailed for Siberia.

He didn't notice that danger sailed with him.

Celia was a dangerous mouse. She was a large jumping mouse who also wanted the Jade Gerbil. Joe was a small mouse, only six centimeters tall.

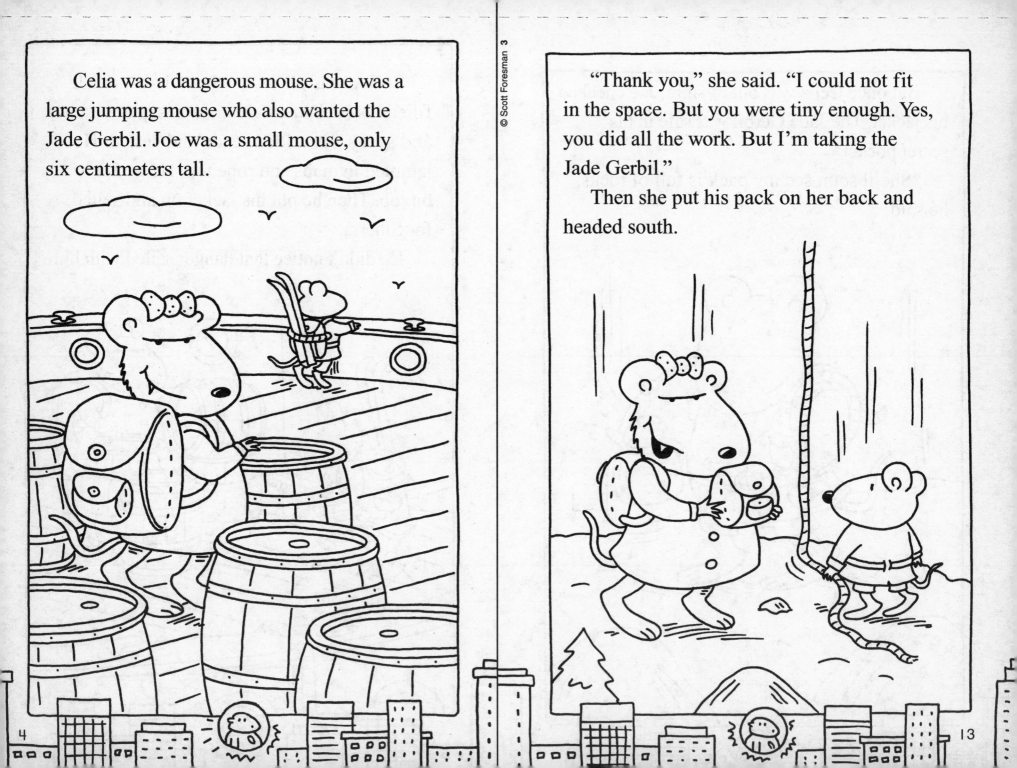

"Thank you," she said. "I could not fit in the space. But you were tiny enough. Yes, you did all the work. But I'm taking the Jade Gerbil."

Then she put his pack on her back and headed south.

When he reached the pass, he looped his rope around a rock. He glided down to safety.

But Celia was waiting for him at the bottom. She just pulled the pack off his back.

The ship landed in an icy harbor. Just as Joe got onto the edge of the dock, a barrel rolled toward him.

Joe jumped out of the way. The barrel missed him, but he dropped his maps and skis.

Celia quickly picked up his maps and skis and took off!

Joe used the barrel to make skis. He followed Celia's tracks.

Something was odd! Celia seemed to be going in a circle. Suddenly Joe knew she was trying to sneak up on him.

But Joe could see the Jade Gerbil in the center of the room.

Joe picked it up. He could tell it was at least a century old. His boss would love it! He headed back.

On the other side of the pass was a crack. Only a six-centimeter-tall jumping mouse could fit into such a tiny space!

Joe went into the crack and crawled into a tiny cave. Its ceiling was low. The room was dark.

He hid beside a pile of rocks. He filled a pair of pants and a shirt with snow. "This looks just like me," he whispered to himself. "Maybe it will trick Celia."

Then he reached into his jacket and pulled out a map. Celia didn't know about his secret pocket.

"This is the real map," he said. "I have to find the Jade Gerbil first!"

Soon he was in the mountains. The rocks were jagged. Ice made the rocks slippery.

He glanced at the map. The Jade Gerbil was on the other side of a pass, so Joe began climbing.

It was quite a job! Joe had to make certain each move was safe. Once or twice he had to use his rope to get to a ledge.

Finally, he reached the pass. There was no sign of Celia.

Scott Foresman
Reading

Grade 3
Phonics Reader 10

**Growing Up in
Colonial Times**
by Linda Lott
illustrated by
Joel Snyder

Phonics Skills:
• Vowel digraph *ow*
• Vowel diphthong *ow*

Scott Foresman
**Phonics
System**

Scott Foresman

Growing Up
in
Colonial Times

by Linda Lott
illustrated by Joel Snyder

This book belongs to

_____

Phonics for Families: This book features words in which the letters *ow* represent the sounds heard at the end of *how* and *know*. Read the book with your child. Then encourage your child to name words that rhyme with *how* and *know*.

Phonics Skills: Vowel digraph *ow*; Vowel diphthong *ow*

Colonial children in New England were always busy. They spent most of their time working and studying. But somehow they always found time to play and have fun.

At the end of the day, the tired children hung their clothes on pegs. Then they crowded into a warm feather bed. They closed their eyes. Tomorrow would be another busy day.

Growing Up in Colonial Times

by Linda Lott
illustrated by Joel Snyder

Scott Foresman

Editorial Offices: Glenview, Illinois • New York, New York
Sales Offices: Reading, Massachusetts • Duluth, Georgia
Glenview, Illinois • Carrollton, Texas • Menlo Park, California

New England Colonies

In the 1700s, most American colonists who lived in the North came from England. They called their colonies New England. Children in these colonies learned to work at an early age. They worked hard. Children helped to get all the work done.

Girls fed the hens in the farmyard. In the spring, they sowed rows and rows of seeds.

In winter, boys were allowed to go skating on frozen ponds. Their skates had wooden blades.

No one ever went sledding in the snow. In colonial times, sledding was against the law. Grown-ups frowned on sledding. Sledding was known as a foolish waste of time.

Girls liked to sew too. They made samplers to show off their best work. With a needle and thread, they drew pictures and wrote words.

Many children made their own clothes too. They spun thread and then wove it into cloth. Both girls and boys picked flowers and berries to make dyes. They used these dyes to color the cloth.

Boys often worked outside. They mowed grassy meadows. They helped their fathers by following plows in the fields. They took care of horses and cows too. Somehow everything got done.

Colonial children also knew how to have fun. They played games like London Bridge and tag.

Boys played with marbles, hoops, and kites. They also liked to throw a feather-filled ball.

Girls had a few dolls. The dolls were made of cornhusks.

© Scott Foresman 3

In colonial times, only a few boys went on to college. Some went home to work on the farm. Others learned to follow a trade. They learned how to be shoemakers or printers. They learned their trades as they worked.

Colonial children knew that it was important to be good. They often read books that told them how to behave. These books even taught them how to stand tall without wiggling.

At dinnertime, grown-ups sat to eat. Children had to stand. Sometimes the children even had to share bowls with brothers and sisters.

Sunday was a quiet day in most New England colonies. It was against the law for children to work or play on Sunday. They could not even sit quietly and build a tower with blocks. On Sunday, children and grown-ups dressed in their best clothes. Sunday was a day to sit and think.

Colonial boys went on to school in town. The school had one room. And it was often cold. The boys crowded together on rows of hard benches.

The teachers were strict. The boys knew they had to follow all the rules.

Most colonial girls didn't go beyond
Dame School. Some families didn't think
this was fair. So some parents taught the
girls on their own.

Sometimes the people got together at
a town meetinghouse. During the winter,
children were allowed to take their dogs
along. The children and dogs would
crowd together to keep warm. The dogs
had to be quiet. They could not howl,
growl, or bark! If they did, they'd soon be
outside in the cold.

Colonial children in New England went to school too. But they went only when their families didn't need them at home.

The youngest children went to Dame School. Dame School was in the teacher's house. Children learned how to read and write at Dame School. They didn't use books. They read from a hornbook.

A hornbook wasn't even a book. It was just a piece of wood. There was a printed page on the front of the wood. Hornbooks lasted a long time.

As soon as the colonial children knew how to read and write, they left Dame School.

Scott Foresman
Reading

Grade 3
Phonics Reader 11

The Wrong Hat
by Babs Bell Hajdusiewicz
illustrated by
Sally Schaedler

Phonics Skill:
• Silent Letters *wr,*
  kn, st, gn, mb

The Wrong Hat

by Babs Bell Hajdusiewicz
illustrated by Sally Schaedler

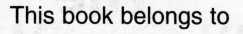

This book belongs to

_____

Phonics for Families: This book gives your child practice reading words that contain silent letters, such as *know, sign, comb, wrong,* and *listen.* Read the book together. Then invite your child to talk about something he or she did that had a surprisingly happy ending.

Phonics Skill: Silent letters *wr, kn, st, gn, mb*

After the game, Mr. Knox took the girls down by the dugout. Carrie wanted to get her ball signed. She couldn't take her eyes off the players.

"I feel better" she said, "now that I'm not wearing the wrong hat!"

The Wrong Hat

by Babs Bell Hajdusiewicz
illustrated by Sally Schaedler

Scott Foresman

Editorial Offices: Glenview, Illinois • New York, New York
Sales Offices: Reading, Massachusetts • Duluth, Georgia
Glenview, Illinois • Carrollton, Texas • Menlo Park, California

Carrie admired herself in her hat
as she waited for Sandra to answer
the phone.

"Sandra!" she said at the sound of her
friend's voice. "Wait until you see what I
got from my uncle! It came just in time
for the game between the Cubs and the
White Sox! I'm glad you invited me!"

"Were you a White Sox fan?" Carrie asked.

"Sure was," said Mr. Knox. "They are a
great team. So, put it on. That hat goes
better with your ball!"

Sandra picked up Carrie's backpack. "Carrie," she said, "you have a White Sox hat to go with your ball!"

"It looks as if you were wearing the wrong hat," said Mr. Knox. "Let's see how this hat looks on you. I used to wear one of those myself."

"I'm glad you are coming," said Sandra. "My grandpa says that bringing you means one more fan for the Cubs! We're taking the next train, so we have to leave now."

"But Sandra!" Carrie cried.

"I have to go, Carrie!" said Sandra. "Grandpa is in the car! He doesn't want to miss the train. We'll pick you up in a few minutes."

Carrie's heart sank. "I'm not for the Cubs!" she muttered. "I thought Sandra knew how much I liked the White Sox! What will I do now?"

Carrie flopped on her bed. "I should have told Sandra," she said. "But if I told her, she might have uninvited me!"

Carrie was ready to catch the ball. She had her glove up in the air. The crowd screamed as the ball landed and bounced right into Carrie's glove!

"I got it!" she yelled. "I got the ball!"

© Scott Foresman 3

By the third inning, Carrie had forgotten her worries. She stood up as one of the White Sox players swung the bat. The crowd yelled, "Foul ball! Heads up!"

Mr. Knox reached for Sandra's glove. As he moved, he knocked Carrie's backpack to the ground.

Carrie gently hung her hat on the doorknob. "It's my first White Sox game ever!" she said. "It would be rude to wear my hat. But I don't want to cheer for the Cubs! It's not fair!"

Carrie looked at the hat on the doorknob when she finished combing her hair. If only I could wear my hat, she thought.

"Maybe I could just take my hat," said Carrie. "No one would know."

Wrigley Field

Mr. Knox and the girls moved quickly. "The sign says that way!" shouted Mr. Knox. "Listen to those Cubs fans, girls! Let's go!"

Carrie counted the White Sox hats as she hurried to keep up. No one knows I'm wearing the wrong hat, she thought.

On the train, Carrie laid her hat on her knee.

"Carrie," said Mr. Knox, "let's see how that
hat looks on you. There! Now you're a real
Cubs fan!"

Carrie tried her best to smile.

"Hop in, Carrie!" called Sandra.

"Hi, Sandra! " said Carrie. "Hi, Mr. Knox!
Thank you for inviting me!"

"We're glad you could come," said
Sandra's grandpa. "You're one more fan for
the Cubs!"

"So what did your uncle send you?" asked Sandra.

Carrie grabbed her backpack. "It's nothing," she said. "I'll show you some other time."

"We can't miss the train," said Mr. Knox. "Sandra, grab that bag on the seat. It's a surprise for you and Carrie."

© Scott Foresman 3

"Open the bag," said Mr. Knox.

Carrie watched as Sandra pulled two Cubs hats from the bag. She groaned silently as Sandra handed her a hat.

"Wow, Grandpa!" shouted Sandra. "I remember these. But I thought you said these hats were too special to wear!"

"They're special hats for two very special Cubs fans!" said Mr. Knox.

Scott Foresman
Reading

Grade 3
Phonics Reader 12

**Proud to Be
a Farm Girl**
by Robin Bloksberg
illustrated
by N. Jo Tufts

Phonics Skill:
• *R*-controlled vowels

Scott Foresman
Phonics
System

Scott Foresman

Proud to Be
a Farm Girl

by Robin Bloksberg
illustrated by N. Jo Tufts

Scott Foresman

Editorial Offices: Glenview, Illinois • New York, New York
Sales Offices: Reading, Massachusetts • Duluth, Georgia
Glenview, Illinois • Carrollton, Texas • Menlo Park, California

This book belongs to

_____

Phonics for Families: This book gives your child practice in reading words that have the same vowel sounds as in *care*, *farm*, *fair*, and *pear*. Read the book together with your child. Then talk about all the food products your family enjoys which are made from milk.

Phonics Skill: *R*-controlled vowels

The best day on the farm this year was my birthday. We had homemade ice cream, made with our cows' milk.

After my party, Mom and Dad took me out to the barn. They gave me my own calf to take care of! Soon I will be able to show her at the county fair, just like Dad did when he was my age.

I sure am proud to be a farm girl!

Proud to Be a Farm Girl

by Robin Bloksberg
illustrated by N. Jo Tufts

Scott Foresman

Editorial Offices: Glenview, Illinois • New York, New York
Sales Offices: Reading, Massachusetts • Duluth, Georgia
Glenview, Illinois • Carrollton, Texas • Menlo Park, California

On our dairy farm, it is barely sunrise when we get up. Sometimes the stars are still out!

I tie back my hair and wear old jeans, so I can help my dad milk the cows.

Dad told me that when he was a boy, Grandpa gave him a baby calf to raise.

Dad took good care of it all year long, and when summer came, he took the calf to the county fair.

Dad won a ribbon for the best calf!

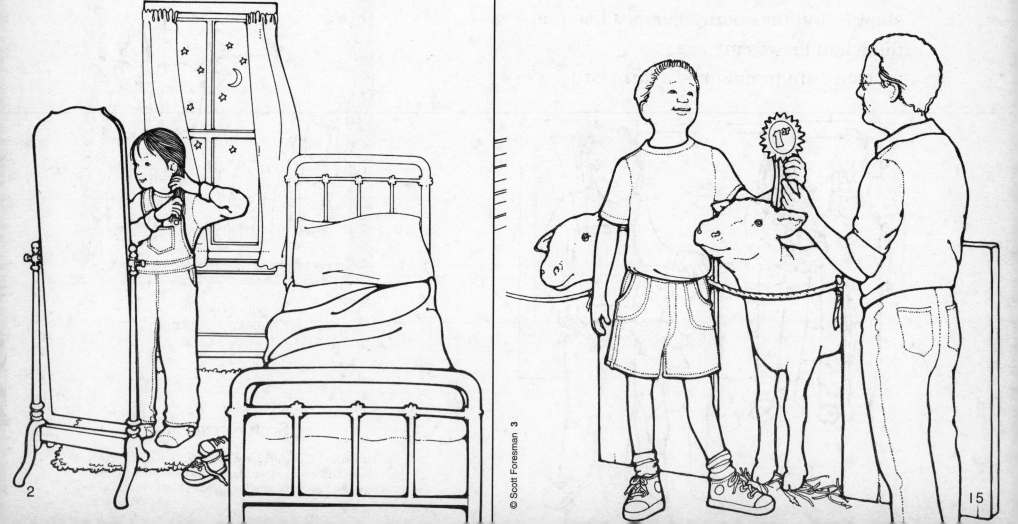

I love having a calf on the farm. It is fun to watch it grow. It's the part of dairy farming that I like best.

Last month, two calves were born on the same day. We barely got to see one calf, before the next one was born! It was amazing to have a pair of newborn calves. Even my baby brother got excited!

The barn is not too far from our farmhouse. I go into the barn with my dad. He calls me his dairy partner!

We start by setting out the things we need. Then Dad attaches the milking machine hoses to the cows.

Our farm has more than 100 Jersey
cows, and we milk them twice a day.
The bigger cows get milked in the
milking parlor.

Dad and I work as a pair, but I do the
easy parts.

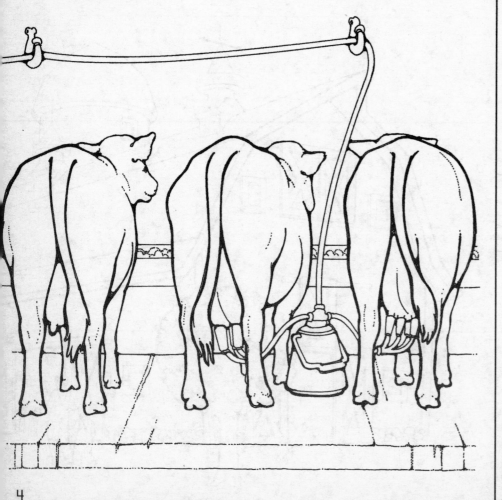

4

Doctor Harris comes if a new calf
needs help. Doc Harris is a veterinarian.
She makes sure all the calves are healthy.

13

Each year on the farm, some of the cows have calves. When it's time, we make a clean space in the barn.

Sometimes Dad stays in the barn in case the cow needs help. Now that I'm nine, sometimes I stay in the barn too. Staying in the barn is fun. We go up the stairs, and sleep in a hayloft. When it's dark, I can see the stars through a hole in the roof.

We milk four cows at a time. Each cow gives over three gallons of milk each day.

Cows love to eat! When we milk them, they eat grain we have harvested. This helps them stay calm during milking.

After the morning milking, it's time for breakfast for us! Sometimes I'm so hungry, I can hardly wait!

Mom cooks a lot of food for dad, my little brother, and me. At the table we talk about our hard work.

When Mom's not looking, I sometime tear off part of my toast and share it with our dog.

When I go to the market with Mom, I see many things made from milk. Some of the milk may even come from our cows!

We buy butter, cheese, yogurt, and my favorite—chocolate marshmallow ice cream. Too bad cows don't give milk that tastes like that!

Every day a dairy truck comes to our farm. The driver parks the truck near the barn, fills the tank with milk, and takes it to the dairy.

If I'm not in school, I sit on a cart and watch.

Sometimes when we eat, Dad tells me about when he was a boy on our farm.

He, my Uncle Carl, and my Aunt Claire grew up here. They didn't have milking machines!

Grandpa would carefully milk all the cows by hand. There were small stools in the milking parlor. Dad had to be careful not to scare the cows!

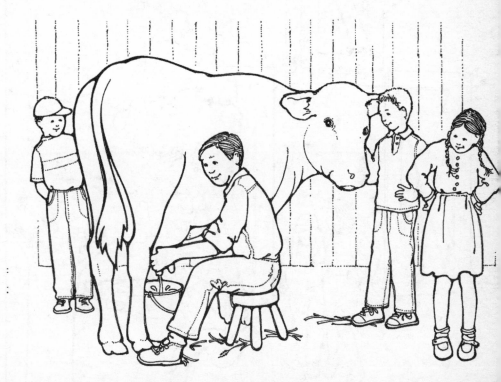

Dad says that milking took longer when he was a boy. He hardly ever got to school on time. First he had to help on the farm, and the old school was very far away.

Sometimes he would take a pear from the tree near the barn, and eat it on the way to school. That pear tree is still on our farm!

I am never late for school. I run down the farmhouse stairs and catch the bus. Sometimes the bus has to wait while Dad takes the cows across the road to the pasture.

The pasture isn't very far. The cows will graze there until it's time for the afternoon milking.

Each cow will eat more than 100 pounds of grass, every day.

© Scott Foresman 3

Scott Foresman
Reading

Grade 3
Phonics Reader 13

AMAZING BUILDINGS
by Anastasia Suen

Phonics Skill:
• Base words

Scott Foresman
Phonics System

Scott Foresman

Amazing Buildings

by Anastasia Suen

This book belongs to

_____

Phonics for Families: This book provides practice reading words, such as *tallest* and *buildings*, which are formed around base words. Invite your child to read the book aloud. Then have him or her name the base words in the story.

Phonics Skill: Base words

PHOTOGRAPHY Cover and Title Page, Joseph Pobereskin/Tony Stone Images; 2, Patrick Ingrand/Tony Stone Images; 3, David Austen/Stock, Boston; 4, Rob Crandall/Stock, Boston; 5, Leonore Weber/Omni-Photo Communications; 6, Dallas and John Heaton/Stock, Boston; 7, John Elk III/Stock, Boston; 9, Johnny Stockshooter/International Stock; 10, Edmund Nagele/International Stock; 11, Pete Seaward/Tony Stone Images; 12, Joseph Pobereskin/Tony Stone Images; 13, Joseph Nettis/Stock, Boston; 14, Nancy L. Fix/Stock, Boston; 15, Steve Benbow/Stock, Boston; 16, Dave Saunders/Tony Stone Images

Sydney Opera House in Sydney, Australia

You can see amazing buildings across the globe. Some are old. Some are new. And others are very tall. What amazing buildings have you seen?

Amazing Buildings

by Anastasia Suen

Scott Foresman

Editorial Offices: Glenview, Illinois • New York, New York
Sales Offices: Reading, Massachusetts • Duluth, Georgia
Glenview, Illinois • Carrollton, Texas • Menlo Park, California

Bodiam Castle, England

What makes a building amazing? Some buildings have existed since ancient times. Other buildings took centuries to build. Still other buildings reach skyward, trying to be the world's tallest.

Petronas Towers in Kuala Lumpur, Malaysia

These are the newest tallest buildings in the world. They were built in 1996. Each tower is eighty-eight stories high. The towers are joined by a bridge at the forty-second floor. How long will they hold the record? Probably not for long! Plans are already in the works for an even taller skyscraper!

Transamerica Pyramid in San Francisco, California

This pyramid is an office building! It was the center of many discussions when it was built in 1972. Buildings in the center of a city usually looked like boxes, not pyramids!

Great Pyramids at Giza, Egypt

These pyramids are one of the Seven Wonders of the Ancient World. They are still standing today. The pyramids are made of rocks. White limestone covered the outside of the pyramids from top to bottom. A special capstone, covered in gold, became the top point.

Temple at Tikal in Guatemala

This pyramid, in Central America, was built about 2,300 years after the Great Pyramids in Egypt. It is made of stone. The walls of the pyramid are covered with limestone, plaster, and paint. This pyramid was rediscovered in 1848.

Sears Tower in Chicago, Illinois

The Sears Tower in Chicago is really nine skyscrapers in one. Bundled together, the towers are of varying sizes. Workers dug a huge trench in the ground and filled it with concrete to make a foundation for the building. This foundation kept the building from sinking. When the Sears Tower was finished in 1974, it became the tallest building in the world.

World Trade Center in New York, New York

Great Wall of China

The twin towers of the World Trade Center in New York City are not the same size. One tower is six feet taller than the other. When they were built, they were the tallest buildings in the world.

Though it is not a building, the Great Wall of China is so large that astronauts can see it from outer space! China's first leader began this construction over two thousand years ago. It continued for hundreds of years. The Great Wall of China is made of earth and stone covered with brick.

The Parthenon in Athens, Greece

Over twenty-two thousand tons of marble were used to make this masterpiece. Each column has eight to ten sections of marble stacked one on top of the other. People still copy the design of these columns today.

Empire State Building in New York, New York

Take an elevator to the top of the Empire State Building and see New York City, a city of skyscrapers. The Empire State Building was called the Eighth Wonder of the World when it opened in 1931. It was the tallest building in the world until the World Trade Center was built in 1972.

Eiffel Tower in Paris, France

This tower, which is made of iron, only took two years to build. It is nearly twice as tall as the Washington Monument.

Anasazi Cliff Palace at Mesa Verde National Park in Colorado

This Cliff Palace in Colorado is in a cave two hundred feet above the ground. It has over two hundred rooms. The builders used sandstone for the walls. They used mud to hold the stones together.

Cathedral in Milan, Italy

This church is one of the largest in the world. Workers began building it around 1386. Work continued for over 500 years. It was not finished until 1887. The church is made of stone.

Taj Mahal in Agra, India

Work on this building began in 1632. Twenty thousand men worked for twenty-two years to build this masterpiece. Covered with white marble, this building seems to change colors with the weather. It also seems to change with the movement of light from the sun and moon.

Scott Foresman
Reading

Grade 3
Phonics Reader 14

The Really Lucky Dog
by Jan M. Mike
illustrated by
Amy Wummer

Phonics Skill:
• Suffixes -ness,
  -ly, -ful, -ous

Scott Foresman
Phonics System

Scott Foresman

The Really Lucky Dog

by Jan M. Mike
illustrated by Amy Wummer

This book belongs to

_____

Phonics for Families: This book gives your child practice reading words with endings such as *-ly, -ness, -ous,* and *-ful.* Have your child read the book aloud and then read together to find the words that have these endings.

Phonics Skill: Suffixes *-ness, -ly, -ful, -ous*

Kareem picked up the shoe and looked
at it carefully. Then he slipped it on and tied
the laces quickly. The shoe was extremely
important to him.

Filled with happiness, he hugged Willy.
"This is my lucky shoe," he whispered.
"And you are my really lucky dog!"

16

The Really Lucky Dog

by Jan M. Mike
illustrated by Amy Wummer

Scott Foresman

Editorial Offices: Glenview, Illinois • New York, New York
Sales Offices: Reading, Massachusetts • Duluth, Georgia
Glenview, Illinois • Carrollton, Texas • Menlo Park, California

Kareem quickly jumped out of bed. His dog, Willy, thumped his tail loudly, but Kareem ignored him. This afternoon was the big soccer game.

Kareem's uniform was neatly folded on the chair. He got dressed. Then he looked under the bed for his soccer shoes.

© Scott Foresman 3

It was Kareem's lucky shoe!

"You found it!" Kareem shouted thankfully.

Willy proudly trotted over and dropped the shoe in front of Kareem. He barked and wagged his tail happily.

Willy jumped off Kareem's bed and began to dig wildly through the blankets in his bed.

"No, not the ball again," Kareem said. "I told you I can't play."

Willy gave a joyous bark. Then he pulled out his prize, but it was not his red ball.

He saw his left shoe, but he couldn't see his right one. Kareem looked again and again. He wasn't successful! No matter how hard he looked, there was only one shoe. His lucky kicking shoe was not under his bed.

"Mom, my shoe is missing!" Kareem yelled loudly.

He looked at the clock. It was late. He was getting nervous. He knew that his parents were busy getting ready for work. He would have to find his shoe by himself. Maybe it was in the poorly lit basement.

Willy jumped up on Kareem's bed and ate the treat. As he ate, Kareem gently petted his soft fur.

His throat felt tight. He really wanted to play in the game. But how could he play with only one shoe?

"Where is my shoe?" he whispered to his dog.

He slowly climbed the stairs. Willy was lying on his dog bed with one paw over his nose. His tail wagged when he saw Kareem.

"I'm truly sorry," Kareem said. "I did not mean to hurt your feelings." He held out a dog treat.

Kareem did not want to go down to the basement alone. The darkness down there scared him.

"Come with me, Willy," he said to his dog. "Come help me find my lucky shoe."

Willy dug playfully in his blankets, where he kept his red ball.

"No!" Kareem said. "I don't want to play ball. Let's go."

He dashed out of the room. Willy was joyful. Together, they raced down the stairs and into the kitchen. Kareem nervously opened the basement door. Darkness hit his eyes.

"I don't like the basement," he whispered. But he had to go down anyway. He had to look for his shoe.

Now Kareem was all alone, with no friend to help him look. He was terribly upset that he had yelled at Willy. Willy was only trying to be playful.

Kareem grabbed a handful of treats and headed upstairs.

"Where is my shoe?" Kareem moaned.

Willy barked and tugged eagerly on Kareem's sleeve. Kareem gently pushed him away.

"You are no help at all. Go to bed, Willy," yelled Kareem.

With his head hanging, Willy slowly walked up the stairs.

Slowly he crept down the stairs, and into the laundry room. He quickly turned on the light and looked around. There was no shoe in the laundry room, or in his father's work room.

"Where is my shoe?" Kareem asked.

Willy barked and tugged gently on Kareem's sleeve.

"No playing, Willy. I have to find my shoe," Kareem said.

They raced upstairs to the kitchen. Willy followed Kareem as he carefully searched the kitchen. He looked under the table, behind the plants, and even in the sink. But there was no sign of his lucky shoe.

8

The living room was next. Kareem searched under the couch and behind the television. He even looked between the books in the big bookcase. There was no shoe anywhere!

He searched and searched the entire house. His lucky shoe had disappeared!

© Scott Foresman 3

9

Scott Foresman
Reading

Grade 3
Phonics Reader 15

Truthful Juan
retold by Jan M. Mike
illustrated by
Jan Naimo Jones

Phonics Skill:
• Medial consonant
  digraphs: *th, ph, sh, ch*

Scott Foresman
Phonics System

Scott Foresman

Truthful Juan

retold by Jan M. Mike
illustrated by Jan Naimo Jones

This book belongs to

_____

Phonics for Families: This book provides practice reading words that contain the letters *th, ph, sh,* and *ch* in the middle of the words. Read this book together. Then help your child make a list of the words that have these medial letter combinations.

Phonics Skill: Medial consonant digraphs *th, ph, sh, ch*

Twelve bright gems lay in the basket. The rancher saw that the boy had not kept even one. He smiled at his old friend.

"Your grandson is a clever, honest boy." He turned to Juan.

"A truthful boy like you will grow up to be a great man. We will use these gems to pay for your education. And someday, everything I own will be yours! But first, let's get some eggs to eat!"

16

Truthful Juan

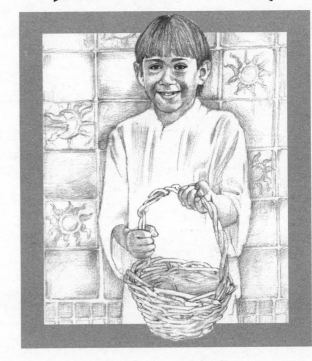

retold by Jan M. Mike
illustrated by Jan Naimo Jones

Scott Foresman

Editorial Offices: Glenview, Illinois • New York, New York
Sales Offices: Reading, Massachusetts • Duluth, Georgia
Glenview, Illinois • Carrollton, Texas • Menlo Park, California

In old Mexico, there lived a rancher who had much land and many horses. He was a rich man in all things, but one. He had no children.

"Are these the eggs that you found?" the rancher asked.

"No, sir." Juan put the basket in front of the rancher and he pulled off the towel.

"A boy told me to trade the eggs for these gems. They are for you. I am sorry you cannot eat them sir. But they are very pretty in the sun."

Juan stood and slowly walked into
the kitchen.

The rancher sat at the kitchen table. He
smiled at the boy. Next to him sat Juan's
grandfather, looking worried.

"Are you all right, Juan?" his grandfather
asked.

Juan nodded.

"Did you find many eggs?"

Juan said, "I found twelve eggs."

One day a poor friend came to visit. The
friend brought his young grandson.

"Grandfather, may I go see the horses?"
the boy asked.

"Of course, but be careful, my Truthful
Juan," his grandfather said.

"My friend, why do you call your grandchild Truthful Juan?" the rancher asked after the boy had left the room.

"He has never told a lie," the poor old grandfather chuckled. "Not even a small one!"

Juan walked slowly into the rancher's house, holding the basket of gems. He found a place to sit. He played with the gems. But their bright glitter made his head hurt. He covered them with a towel, wishing that he had kept the eggs.

Finally his grandfather called him.

"Juan, my Truthful Juan, come bring the eggs to my friend, the rancher."

© Scott Foresman 3

"What shall I tell the rancher?" Juan asked. "He will want to eat his eggs."

"Tell him anything," the older boy said. "Tell him that the eggs broke, or that the chickens did not lay any. You are known as Truthful Juan. Everyone trusts you."

"That cannot be!" the rancher said. "Anyone will lie sometime. No one is truthful all the time."

"Not my Juan," the grandfather said.

"This is what we'll do," the rancher said. "If I find the boy has told a lie, then you must sell me your best horse."

The grandfather was silent. He trusted his grandson. But the thought of losing his best horse began to bother him.

"What will happen if he does not lie?" he asked.

"I will leave him everything I own," the rich rancher said.

Juan looked at his basket of eggs. Then he looked at the sparkling gems. He had never seen so many gems. He knew he should not trade the eggs away. They didn't belong to him. But the gems were so pretty. He wanted to hold them.

Juan handed the boy his basket of eggs. He took the basket of gems in his shaking hands.

© Scott Foresman 3

"Give me your eggs, and I will give you
what is in my basket," the boy said.

He held out a large basket. Juan saw that
it was filled with bright gems, sparkling in
the sunshine.

"Take them," the boy said. "You can bring
them home. Your grandfather will be so happy
when you are both rich!"

So it was agreed. Juan and his grandfather
went to bed. The rancher went into his trophy
room. He reached into his safe, and picked out
twelve bright gems. He put them in a wicker
basket. Then he called for a servant boy.

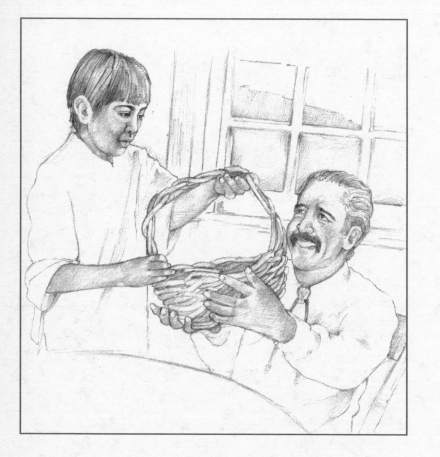

The next morning the rancher smiled at Truthful Juan as he came into the kitchen.

"Will you help me, Juan? I need someone to gather eggs from the chickens," said the rancher.

"Yes, sir. I like to gather eggs," said Juan.

Then the rancher handed Juan a basket.

Juan ran off to the chicken house. He filled the basket with warm brown eggs. As he walked out into the sunshine, the servant grabbed his arm.

"What do you have in your basket?" the servant asked.

"Eggs," Juan said.

© Scott Foresman 3

Scott Foresman
Reading

Grade 3
Phonics Reader 16

Animal Tracks
by Stacey Sparks
illustrated by
Ron Barrett

Phonics Skill:
• Initial and final
  consonant blends

Scott Foresman
Phonics
System

Scott Foresman

Animal Tracks

by Stacey Sparks
illustrated by Ron Barrett

This book belongs to

_____

Phonics for Families: This book will give your child practice in reading words that begin or end with two-letter consonant blends, such as *sl*, *fl*, *ld*, and *nt*. Read the book together with your child. Then go outside and try to find and identify some animal tracks around your home.

Phonics Skill: Initial and final consonant blends

You can find animal tracks in your
yard or in a park. You can find them in
the sand at the beach. You can find them
in damp grass and in dry dust. You can
find them in mud and in snow.

Start looking. You'll see.

16

Animal Tracks

by Stacey Sparks
illustrated by Ron Barrett

Scott Foresman

Editorial Offices: Glenview, Illinois • New York, New York
Sales Offices: Reading, Massachusetts • Duluth, Georgia
Glenview, Illinois • Carrollton, Texas • Menlo Park, California

This boy loves animals. He knows they live all around him. They are in the field and in the woods and in the pond.

There are many good books about animal tracks. You can find them in stores and libraries. They have pictures of many kinds of tracks. They also tell you the best places to look for animal footprints. If you study these books, you too can read the clues that animals leave behind.

The boy steps into his own backyard.
A pair of tracks leads to his house. One
set is round, with no claw marks
showing. The other set has a claw mark
at the end of each toe.

The round mark was made by the
boy's cat. The other mark was made by
his dog. The cat waits for him by the
door, and the dog looks out through the
window. They are not shy like wild
animals. They are glad he is back.

It is hard to see them. Some of them
blend in with the snow. Some are hiding
under the ground or up in trees. Others
are just very tiny. But the boy is smart. He
knows how to find clues that show where
the animals have been.

The boy is looking for animal tracks.
He has just found some in the snow. He
stares at them. He says to himself, "A
snowshoe hare was here."

A snowshoe hare is a kind of rabbit.
Its hind feet are much bigger than its
front feet. When the snowshoe hare
moves, its hind feet land before its front
feet. No other animal leaves a footprint
quite like this one.

The boy has left the pond. Is he scared
that he will meet the skunk?

No. The boy knows that skunks sleep
during the daytime. They will not bother
anyone on this winter day.

The boy is going home because he is
cold. He wants something hot to drink.

It's too bad. He should have walked a
little farther. He just missed seeing the
tracks that the deer left behind. He also
missed seeing the deer!

Otter

Mink

What is this other track next to the beaver print? First the boy must count the number of toes. He counts five. An otter has five toes, but its tracks are bigger than this one. A mink has five toes, but each toe ends in a sharp point.

The print on the ground belongs to an animal you don't want to get too close to. It was made by a skunk!

Now the boy has spotted some more tracks. They look like tiny dots. Whatever made them must be very small. The boy bends down to see them better. He sees a line between each set of the footprints. Now he knows what walked here.

It was a mouse. The mouse's tail dragged in the snow and made the lines. The boy sees the tracks, but he still does not see the mouse.

The boy spies another set of tracks.
They are heading over to the tree. From
where he is standing, they look like
rabbit prints. The boy follows the trail.

Yes! The boy has found a beaver
track. He is pleased because these tracks
are hard to find. A beaver has a big, flat
tail. When it walks, the tail drags behind
and often rubs out the beaver's footprints.

Most of the time, a track is a clue. It can lead you to an animal or an animal's home. Sometimes it's the other way around. Seeing an animal's home can help you find a track.

In the middle of the pond there is a mound of sticks. Beavers piled up these sticks to make a dam. The boy looks at the dam. Then he stares down at the mud again.

Up close, the boy can see the prints better. The front track has four toes. The hind track has five toes. This trail was not made by a rabbit. It was made by a squirrel.

The boy wants to know if it was made by a gray or red squirrel. He takes a ruler out of his pocket to check. The hind track is about one-inch long. That means it was made by a red squirrel. A gray squirrel has a bigger foot.

The boy walks along the track. The snow crunches under his feet. The boy is starting to get cold, but he is happy. The tracks have led him to the squirrel's nest. The squirrel looks down at him and chatters. The boy looks up and smiles at the squirrel.

"It's okay," says the boy. "I'm not trying to get you. I just wanted to see where you live."

The boy walks over to the pond. Next to the water, some of the snow has started to melt. There are tracks in the soft mud. Each track looks like a tiny hand. The boy thinks out loud, "What made these tracks?"

The boy smiles. He knows what kind of animal has toes that look like fingers. A raccoon was here—probably last night. The boy knows he will not see the raccoon. Raccoons like to rest during the day.

Scott Foresman
Reading

Grade 3
Phonics Reader 17

**The Splash on
Spring Street**
by Bill E. Neder
illustrated by
Nina Laden

Phonics Skill:
• Three-letter blends

Scott Foresman
**Phonics
System**

Scott Foresman

The Splash on Spring Street

by Bill E. Neder
illustrated by Nina Laden

This book belongs to

_____

Phonics for Families: This book gives your child practice in reading words that begin with the three-letter blends *str*, *spr*, *spl*, *scr*, *squ*, and *thr*. After reading the book together, have your child go back through the story and find the words that begin with the three-letter blends.

Phonics Skill: Three-letter blends

The next day, the three judges held up the squirrel's painting.

"Who painted this picture?" they asked. "It has won first prize, but there is no name on it. Raise your hand if it is yours."

No one raised a hand. The three judges looked at each other. "How strange!" they said.

Of course, you know who won! So if you ever see that squirrel with the painted tail, tell him to go to the Stream Square Mall. His prize is still waiting for him!

16

The Splash on Spring Street

by Bill E. Neder
illustrated by Nina Laden

Scott Foresman

Editorial Offices: Glenview, Illinois • New York, New York
Sales Offices: Reading, Massachusetts • Duluth, Georgia
Glenview, Illinois • Carrollton, Texas • Menlo Park, California

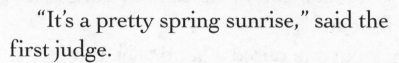

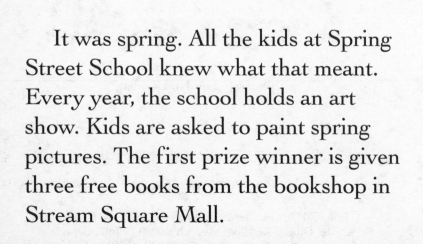

It was spring. All the kids at Spring Street School knew what that meant. Every year, the school holds an art show. Kids are asked to paint spring pictures. The first prize winner is given three free books from the bookshop in Stream Square Mall.

"It's a pretty spring sunrise," said the first judge.

"No, no! It's a bird's nest!" said another.

"You're both wrong!" said the third judge. "It is clearly a spring field!"

Each judge saw the picture in a different way. Yet all three judges felt that it was the best work of all!

© Scott Foresman 3

That day, three judges looked at the artwork. When they came to the squirrel's painting, one judge cried, "What a strange picture!"

"Yes," said another. "Such strange splashes of paint! Yet it is very good!"

"What do you think it is?" asked the third judge.

At school, friends talked about their plans.

"I'm going to paint spring birds," Tom said.

"I plan to paint spring flowers," said Jill.

"I think I'll paint a lake or stream," Dan said.

After school, Tom went straight home to start on his art. He took a big, square sheet of paper. He sat by the back door and looked through the screen. There were three birds in the backyard. One bird was sitting on a straw. Another bird squeaked a sweet song. The third bird spread and stretched its wings.

The next morning, Jill found the strange painting.

"How did this get here?" Jill thought. "Maybe Tom or Dan dropped it on the way to school."

Jill took the painting to school, along with her own picture. She put them both in the box for all the artwork.

The squirrel squirmed and squirmed.
His tail landed in the wet paint. Splash!
Then the squirrel sprang onto the paper.
His tail struck again. Splat!

Splash! Splat! Splash! Splat! The
wet tail struck the paper again and
again. It worked just like a paintbrush!
Soon, a strange picture started to form!

Tom went to work. He used paint
that came in tubes. As he squeezed
each tube, paint squirted onto the
paper. Tom spread the paint with the
flat side of a knife. Then he scraped off
the paint that he didn't want. His father
had taught him to paint that way.

Soon, Tom had painted all the birds.
When he was through, he looked at his
work. He was thrilled. "My art is going
to win!" Tom thought.

Next door, Jill was outside painting her picture. She sat near a bed of flowers. They had sprung up tall and straight. They were red, yellow, green, blue, pink, and white. "What a pretty picture this will make!" Jill thought.

That night, a squirrel ran through the flower bed. Some scraps of thread and string were trapped on his tail. The squirrel began to squirm as he tried to get the thread and string off his tail.

The squirrel's tail hit the paint jars. They all fell over! Wet paint spread all over the ground!

© Scott Foresman 3

During the night, something very strange took place on Spring Street. Jill had brought her painting inside, but she had not remembered her paint jars, her brushes, or her paper! They were still outside by the flowers.

Jill's paint was in jars. She dipped her brush into a jar and then dragged it across the paper. She made pretty stripes. Sometimes she splashed paint in spots.

When she was through, Jill was thrilled. "I have a very strong feeling I will win!" Jill said.

Dan also began to work on his picture. There was no lake or stream near his home on Spring Street. So he strolled with his dad to a nearby stream.

© Scott Foresman 3

Dan used cans of spray paint. He pressed the button at the top of the can. Paint sprayed out onto the paper. Dan sprayed just where he wanted the paint to go. Sometimes a little paint would streak, but Dan didn't care.

When he was through, Dan was thrilled. "My art has got to win!" he screamed.

Scott Foresman
Reading

Grade 3
Phonics Reader 18

Cowboys on the Trail
by Lee S. Justice
illustrated by
Den Schofield

Phonics Skill:
• Vowel diphthongs
  oi and *oy*

Scott Foresman
Phonics System

Scott Foresman

Cowboys on the Trail

by Lee S. Justice
illustrated by Den Schofield

This book belongs to

_____

Phonics for Families: This book gives your child practice in reading words with *oi* and *oy*, as in *noise* and *boy*. After your child reads the book aloud to you, ask him or her to point out and say the words with *oi* and *oy*.

Phonics Skill: Vowel diphthongs *oi* and *oy*

Cowboys still worked hard on the ranches.
They still roped and rode with skill. They still
sang their songs. But there were no more days
and nights of herding on the long trails north.

Cowboys on the Trail

by Lee S. Justice

illustrated by Den Schofield

Scott Foresman

Editorial Offices: Glenview, Illinois • New York, New York
Sales Offices: Reading, Massachusetts • Duluth, Georgia
Glenview, Illinois • Carrollton, Texas • Menlo Park, California

Long ago in Texas, cattle roamed free on the open range. They were wild and strong. They could eat almost any kind of grass or plant without getting sick. These cattle had long legs and long horns. They were called Texas longhorns.

For about twenty years, cowboys drove Texas longhorns north on the dusty trails. Then ranchers began to fence in their land. The open range was gone.

Sometimes a trail drive lasted three long months! When it ended, cowboys enjoyed spending time in town.

In Texas, a longhorn cow could be sold for about four dollars. That was not much money. But people in the East were willing to pay forty dollars for the same cow! If Texas longhorns could be shipped to the East, then cattle owners could make more money. But there was a big problem.

At that time, there were no railroads in Texas. There was no way to ship the cattle to the East. Or was there?

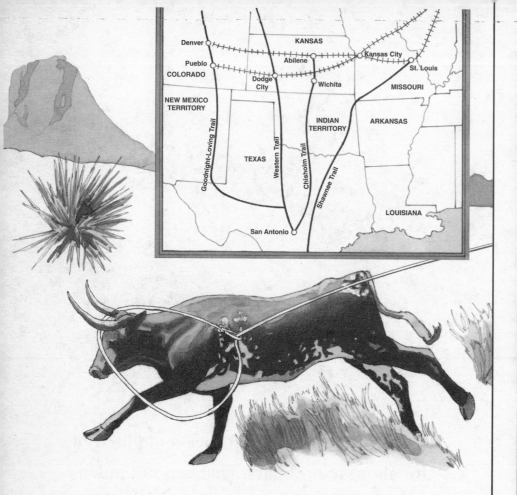

The cattle owners of Texas found a way to ship longhorns to markets in the East. Railroads reached into some towns north of Texas. Those towns became shipping points. Men on horseback herded the cattle north from Texas. The herders on horseback were called cowboys.

A cowboy could not sleep long. At night, he took a turn watching the herd. Cowboys on night watch rode around the herd. They kept the animals together and sang them to sleep. The cowboys sang in gentle voices. Their songs were often about hard work on the trail.

Cowboys took turns at different jobs. The pointers rode up front. They pointed the leading longhorns in the right direction. Other cowboys herded from the sides. The drag riders rode at the rear. They herded the slowest longhorns through clouds of dust.

Cowboys drove the cattle across rivers. They pulled animals out of mud. From sunrise to sunset, the cowboys kept the cattle on the trail.

In the spring, cowboys from many ranches joined together. They spread out over many miles of open range. They roped thousands of longhorns and herded them together.

At the spring roundup, the cattle owners chose cattle that would take the long trip north. They chose a trail boss to lead the cattle drive.

The trail boss hired the cowboys to drive the cattle north. He also hired a cook and a wrangler.

The cook was in charge of the chuck wagon. It held water, pots, firewood, and tools. It also held food. Food on the trail was not fancy. There were lots of boiled beans.

The wrangler was in charge of the horses. A wrangler was often a young boy.

© Scott Foresman 3

The greatest danger of all was a stampede. Any sudden noise could scare the longhorns. The animals would then dash off at top speed. The cowboys would have to race to the head of the herd. Then they would try to force the running cattle into a circle. A horse and rider could easily be crushed in a stampede!

Cowboys were brave. They faced so many dangers on the trail.

Cowboys herded cattle through dust storms and broiling heat. They herded across open land when lightning flashed all around.

Cowboys had to be aware of rattlesnakes that might be coiled nearby. They had to look out for hidden holes that might cause a horse to stumble and fall.

Cowboys just had to learn how to deal with some dangers. They had to learn how to avoid others.

Who were the cowboys on the trail? They were strong, young men. They were expert riders and ropers. All had made the choice to work at one of the hardest jobs in the West.

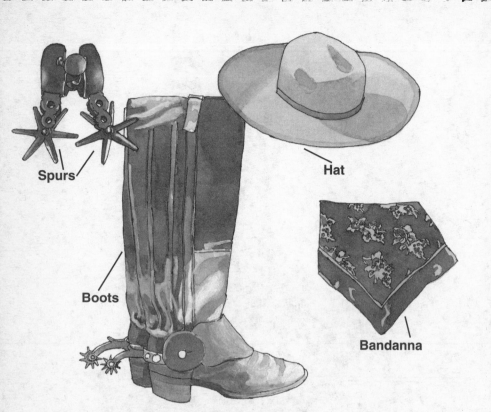

Spurs

Hat

Boots

Bandanna

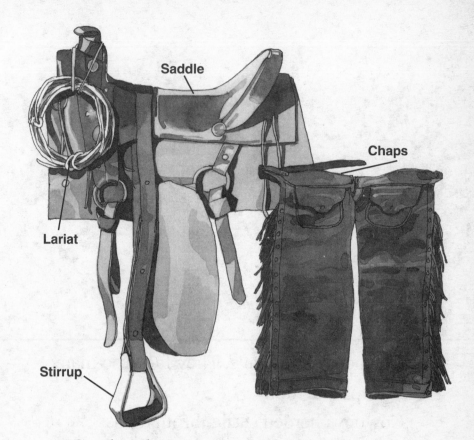

Saddle

Chaps

Lariat

Stirrup

A cowboy could not bring many things on the trail. But there were some things he needed. One of them was a hat. Its wide brim gave shade in the broiling sun. It also kept the rain off the cowboy's face. A hat could fan a fire. It could hold water too.

A cowboy wore leather or fur chaps to protect his legs and pants. His bandanna could protect his mouth and nose when dust filled the air.

Cowboy boots were made for riding. Pointed toes and high heels helped the feet slip into the stirrups and stay there. Spurs on the heels helped control a horse.

The most important thing that a cowboy owned was his saddle. After all, he spent most of his time in it! The saddle had a horn for holding his most important tool—his lariat (LAR-ree-it).

© Scott Foresman 3

Scott Foresman
Reading

Grade 3
Phonics Reader 19

**My New Friend's
Noodles**
by Robin Bloksberg
illustrated by
Anni Matsick

Phonics Skill:
• Possessives (singular
  and plural)

Scott Foresman
**Phonics
System**

Scott Foresman

My New Friend's
Noodles

by Robin Bloksberg
illustrated by Anni Matsick

This book belongs to

_____

Well, almost no one!

My New Friend's Noodles

by Robin Bloksberg
illustrated by Anni Matsick

Scott Foresman

Editorial Offices: Glenview, Illinois • New York, New York
Sales Offices: Reading, Massachusetts • Duluth, Georgia
Glenview, Illinois • Carrollton, Texas • Menlo Park, California

Last week my best friend, Beth, told me that she and her family were moving. She said her dad's job was the reason they had to move.

As I walked up to her house today, I started to think about all the great times we had together. Beth's mom saw me coming and opened the door.

"Hello, Nicole," she said. "Beth is upstairs in her room." I quickly ran up the stairs.

"I don't want anyone new moving into your family's house," I told Beth. "If I can't have you next door, than I don't want anyone!"

May and I have become good friends. I still miss my old friend Beth, but it's been fun making a new friend. And May's mother's noodles are the best!

May has been teaching me how to speak a little Chinese. And I've been helping her with her English, even though she's already good at it.

May is teaching me how to write in Chinese too. Then we can write notes and letters to each other. And no one else will know what we're saying.

That night, as we ate Mom's delicious dinner, I told my parents about May's life in China. Living in another country sounded great to me, I told them.

"You know, my mother's grandparents came from Italy," my mother said.

I didn't know that.

"My grandmother was born in Finland," said Dad.

That sounded pretty exciting to me.

The next few weeks, Beth and I watched people come to look at Beth's house. A family in a blue van came back three times. Each time, the parents went into the house with two little boys.

"I hope this doesn't turn into a boys' neighborhood," I said to Beth.

"But look in the family's van," Beth said. "There's also a girl, and she looks our age."

"She doesn't look as if she wants to live someplace new," I said.

"I know how she feels," Beth said as she hugged me.

Not long after Beth's family moved out of their house, a new family moved in. It was the family with the blue van.

Summer was over and school was about to start. Here I was in third grade, and my best friend had moved away. It was a good thing that Beth's letters were arriving every day.

I noticed that on many days, the mailman also had mail for the new girl next door. She probably had a friend somewhere else too.

Then I asked May if she'd write her name in Chinese for me. She went to her father's desk, and found a brush, some ink, and a piece of paper that May said was made of rice.

May wrote her name with the brush, writing from the top to the bottom. Then she wrote her brothers' names.

I asked her to write my name in those beautiful brush strokes, and she did.

© Scott Foresman 3

I asked May to tell me about China. She told me about her family's apartment, and her friends, and her school.

May went and got her father's book of maps, called an atlas, and showed me where she lived in China.

I asked May to say something in Chinese. Then I asked her what she said.

"I like my new American friend, Nicole," she said.

On the first day of school, the new girl and her mother came to the bus stop. I could tell by the girl's face that she was nervous.

None of the other children said anything to the girl, so I said "hello." She looked shy, but she finally said "hi" back. I asked her what her name was.

She said, "I'm May Ling, but you can call me May."

Then the bus came. Before we got on, May's mother handed her a shiny lunch box.

It turned out that May was in my class at school. Our teacher told everyone in the class that May was a new student. May's family is from China, and they came here because of her dad's new job.

After school, I changed into my play clothes and told my mother I was going to May's house.

"She's the new girl next door," I reminded her.

"That's nice!" she said. "Do you mind if I go with you? I've been meaning to go say hello and welcome them to the neighborhood."

So she took my brother's hand and we all went next door.

My mother, my brother, and May's mother talked in the kitchen. May and I ran upstairs to her room, which used to be Beth's room.

I tried to use chopsticks once at a restaurant. After I dropped more food on the floor than went into my mouth, I gave up.

May made eating with chopsticks look so easy. I really wanted to give it another try. I asked May to show me how to use them. May put the chopsticks into my hand and made me close my fingers, sort of like a crab's claw. She told me to pretend to eat her noodles with the chopsticks. I was able to do it!

At recess, I played hopscotch with some of my friends. May didn't play. She just watched.

After awhile, I noticed that May's face looked sad. I went and asked if she wanted to join us.

It turned out that she didn't know how to play. So I showed her.

"Someday I'll show you some of my friends' favorite games from China," said May.

After recess, the teacher's plan was to have each of us take a turn reading out loud. When it was May's turn, she spoke softly and her words didn't sound quite right.

When we were getting ready for lunch, I told May I would help her with English, if she would help me learn to speak Chinese. May was thrilled that I wanted to learn Chinese.

At lunch, I asked May if she wanted to eat with me and my friend Emily. May said yes, and sat down with us.

I had my favorite sandwich—cold meat loaf. Emily's mother had packed her favorite lunch—a cheese and tomato sandwich, with no crust.

May opened her lunch box, and inside was a bowl with noodles and vegetables. She started eating them with chopsticks. You should have seen the children's faces when they saw that!

8

9

Scott Foresman
Reading

Grade 3
Phonics Reader 20

**Why Mosquitoes
Buzz In People's Ears**
retold by Judy Veramendi
illustrated by
Nan Brooks

Phonics Skill:
• *R*-controlled vowels

Scott Foresman
**Phonics
System**

Scott Foresman

Why Mosquitoes
Buzz in
People's Ears

retold by Judy Veramendi
illustrated by Nan Brooks

This book belongs to

_____

Phonics for Families: This book gives your child practice reading words in which the letter *r* changes the sound of the vowel, as in *before, floor, course, cheerful, hear, search, girl,* and *her.* Read the book together. Then have your child go back through the story and find the words in which the letter *r* controls the sound of the vowel.

Phonics Skill: *R*-controlled vowels

The animals searched and searched for the mosquito, but they could not find her.

Since then, the mosquito lives in fear. To this day, she goes about buzzing in people's ears, "Is everyone still angry at me?"

And they always give her the same answer: "Smack!"

16

Why Mosquitoes Buzz in People's Ears

retold by Judy Veramendi
illustrated by Nan Brooks

Scott Foresman

Editorial Offices: Glenview, Illinois • New York, New York
Sales Offices: Reading, Massachusetts • Duluth, Georgia
Glenview, Illinois • Carrollton, Texas • Menlo Park, California

One morning a mosquito saw a lizard
in the forest. The mosquito said, "Lizard,
I want to tell you about something I saw
this morning."

The lizard looked bored.

The mosquito said, "I saw a girl picking
yams that were almost as big as I am."

"I never heard such a silly thing before!"
said the lizard. "Tell me no more!"

The lizard stuck two sticks in his ears
and hurried away through the forest.

who scared the rabbit,
who alarmed the bird,
who alerted the monkey,
who almost hurt the owls,
and now Mother Owl won't hoot for the
sun so morning can come."

"Search for the mosquito!" roared all
the animals.

When Mother Owl heard that, she felt
more cheerful. She turned her head to the
east and hooted.

And morning appeared.

"Then why didn't you say good morning to me?" asked the snake.

"I couldn't hear you! I put sticks in my ears so I wouldn't hear the mosquito's horrible stories."

King Lion roared with laughter. "So that's why you had sticks in your ears!"

"Of course!" said the lizard.

The King said to the circle of animals, "Therefore, it was the mosquito who upset the lizard, who ignored the snake,

Before long the lizard passed by his friend the snake.

"Good morning," said the snake.

But the lizard ignored the snake, for he couldn't hear him. He still had the sticks in his ears.

The snake was upset. "The lizard has never ignored me before. He must be planning to do something to me."

The snake searched for a place to hide. He slithered into a rabbit hole. "I'll be safe in this place," he said.

When the rabbit saw the snake going into her hole, she scurried out the back door. She ran into a clearing in the forest.

A large bird saw the rabbit hurrying across the forest floor. The bird knew something must be wrong. It was the bird's job to alert the forest animals in case of danger. So he flew through the forest crying the alert.

A monkey heard the bird. He was sure some enormous beast was nearby.

He jumped from the forest floor into the trees to help alert the other animals.

© Scott Foresman 3

Now the King called for the lizard. But he didn't appear because he could not hear.

So the long-eared fox went to search for him, and brought him before the king.

All the animals laughed when they saw the lizard with sticks in his ears.

King Lion pulled out the sticks. Then he asked, "Lizard, why did you ignore the snake? You hurt his feelings."

"What?" asked the lizard. "I would never hurt the snake. He is my friend."

The snake came before the King and said, "King! I said good morning to the lizard, but he ignored me. So I hid."

The King said,
"Therefore, it was the lizard
who ignored the snake,
who scared the rabbit,
who alarmed the bird,
who alerted the monkey,
who almost hurt the owls,
and now Mother Owl won't hoot for the sun so morning can come."

Unfortunately the monkey landed on a dead tree branch, which broke and fell on a bird's nest.

The nest belonged to Mother Owl. She was out searching for food for her baby birds. When she returned to the nest, she learned that the monkey had landed on her nest and almost hurt her babies.

She was so upset. She sat and cried, all day and all night.

Mother Owl normally woke the sun each day so morning would come.

But now, she was too upset. She did not hoot for the sun and morning did not come. The animals of the forest feared it would never come. They called for King Lion.

Soon King Lion appeared. He called for a meeting of all the animals of the forest.

They came and sat in a circle before him.

Mother Owl did not appear, so King Lion sent a long-eared fox to search for her.

"King," said the rabbit, "it was the snake who filled me with fear. He slithered into my hole."

The King said,
"Therefore, it was the snake
who scared the rabbit,
who alarmed the bird,
who alerted the monkey,
who almost hurt the owls,
and now Mother Owl won't hoot for the sun so morning can come."

So, King Lion called for the snake.

The King said to the circle of animals,
"Therefore, it was the rabbit
who alarmed the bird,
who alerted the monkey,
who almost hurt the owls,
and now Mother Owl won't hoot for the
sun so morning can come."

Then King Lion called for the rabbit.
The poor little animal appeared nervous.

"Rabbit," the King said sternly, "why
did you run across the forest floor in the
clear morning light?"

The fox brought Mother Owl before the
King. "Mother Owl, why haven't you
hooted for the sun?" asked the King.
"Morning has not appeared, and all the
animals of the forest are nervous."

Mother Owl said, "Monkey almost
hurt my babies. I am too sad to hoot for
the sun."

King Lion called for the monkey.

The monkey appeared, nervously looking around.

"Monkey," asked the King, "why did you hurt the baby owls?"

"King," said the monkey, "it was the bird's fault. She called an alert through the forest. I thought some enormous beast was near, and I went leaping through the branches of the trees to help spread the alert. A dead branch broke under me, and I fell on the owl's nest."

The King said to the circle of animals, "Therefore, it was the bird who alerted the monkey, who almost hurt the baby owls, and now Mother Owl won't hoot for the sun so morning can come."

Then the King called for the bird. The bird appeared before him and said, "King, it was the rabbit who first alarmed me. I saw her hurrying across the forest floor in the clear light of morning. So I alerted the other animals."

© Scott Foresman **3**

Grade 3
Phonics Reader 21

A Tale of Two Slugs
by Sydnie Meltzer
Kleinhenz
illustrated by
Eldon Doty

Phonics Skill:
• Plurals (regular and
  irregular)

A Tale
of Two Slugs

by Sydnie Meltzer Kleinhenz
illustrated by Eldon Doty

This book belongs to

_____

Phonics for Families: This book gives your child practice reading words that indicate plurals, such as *slugs, tales, bodies, leaves,* and *children*. After enjoying the story together, have your child look around the room and point and identify plural objects, such as chairs, pens, windows, and books.

Phonics Skill: Plurals (regular and irregular)

Buddy and Squig slid off the porch. They hurried under the leaves in the garden.

"Whew!" Squig said. "We're safe!"

"You know what the wise old slugs say," Buddy said. " 'Better safe than squashed!' "

"That was too much of an adventure for me," Squig said.

Buddy took a bite of a green leaf. "Let's just hunt leaves," he said between chews.

Squig laughed. "Okay, Boss. I'll take mine unsalted!"

A Tale of Two Slugs

by Sydnie Meltzer Kleinhenz
illustrated by Eldon Doty

Scott Foresman

Editorial Offices: Glenview, Illinois • New York, New York
Sales Offices: Reading, Massachusetts • Duluth, Georgia
Glenview, Illinois • Carrollton, Texas • Menlo Park, California

A big slug slid out from under a pile of wet leaves and onto the porch step. A little slug followed close behind.

"Caution! Danger zone!" yelled the little slug, but the big one kept going. "Stop, Squig! You know what the wise old slugs say."

"Learn the slime tales, Buddy," said Squig. He continued to push forward.

© Scott Foresman 3

The boy's feet pounded the ground as he ran on out the door onto the porch. There, he stopped to zip his jacket.

"Let's get out of here!" Buddy said.

The slugs got their feet on the ground only moments before the boy ran down the steps.

"Hurry!" Buddy said. "Squeeze in!"
Squig didn't have the breath to answer.

They had just slipped out of sight when the boy sat on their slime trails. He quickly put on his soccer shoes, and jumped up.

"See you later, Mom. I'm going to the field to play soccer," he said.

"Bye," said the mom. Then she bent down to the floor. "Now where did those slugs go? Their trails just stop!"

"It's true about humans," Buddy said. "They can make us as flat as a mat with one step. How can little one-footed slugs get away from their two big feet?"

Squig slowed down. "I'm hunting for a little adventure, and this looks like a good place to find it. I promise I'll keep my eyes open for humans."

He started up the shoe.

Buddy felt the ground shake. He swung his eyes and saw the thing that he feared most.

"Squig, don't! Stop!" Buddy yelled as he scooted to catch Squig. At that moment, a human's fingers lifted the shoe, leaving Buddy dangling from Squig's foot.

© Scott Foresman 3

Buddy and Squig slid to the shoes as fast as they could.

"How can this work?" asked Squig.

"Do as the wise old slugs say," panted Buddy. Suddenly he saw the shoes in a new way. "Follow me," he told Squig.

Buddy scooted between the bumps on the bottom of the shoe. "The human is on our trail so we have to hide," said Buddy.

A boy walked into the room.

Buddy and Squig froze. They watched the human bend down to the floor and blink its eyes near their eyes.

Buddy sighed. Squig wailed, "Now what do we do?"

The woman squealed. "Slugs! Gross! I have to get rid of them. I need something to pick them up." Her big feet shook the floor as she left the room.

"Crank up the slime," Buddy ordered. "Move quickly!"

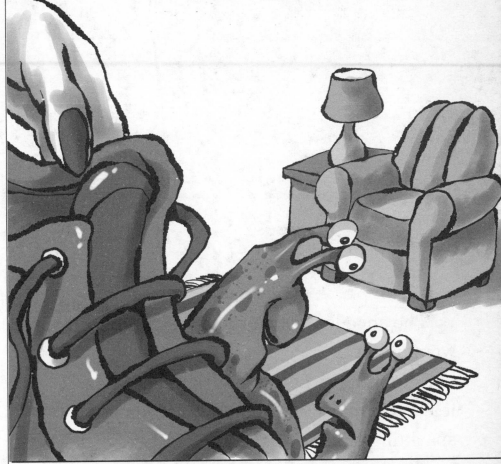

"Buddy! I'm glad you stuck around," Squig said as he was enjoying the ride.

Buddy squirmed closer. "I'm trying to save you, Squig."

Squig shrugged his feelers. "I thought you were telling me, 'Don't stop!'"

The slugs rode into the house on the side of a soccer shoe.

The shoe landed on the floor and the woman left.

"I'm hungry. Let's see if this place has leaves," Squig said. He and Buddy made sparkling slime trails as they slid.

"We have to go home," Buddy said. "You know what the wise old slugs say. 'Don't go sticking your feelers into other folks' business.'"

"You're still little. Children have much to learn," said Squig. "I've been around two summers, so you can trust me. I know we'll be fine."

Buddy sighed and blinked his blurry eyes. "Get back up on your foot," he begged Squig. "We have to go home."

"How?" Squig asked weakly.

Buddy had to think for a moment. Then he softly spoke the answer to Squig's question. "The wise old slugs say, 'Go back the way you came.'"

Suddenly, the floor shook.

"You need water, quick," Buddy said as he looked high and low. "I see some water. Come on Squig."

"I can't move, Buddy. It burns," cried Squig.

Squig was big, but he didn't have much sticky slime left. Buddy rolled him over and over to the water on the floor near the dog's bowl.

Squig stopped talking. His body was curled up and still. Buddy dipped his feelers in the water and patted them on Squig. Slowly Squig stretched.

"Feet! Feet!" Buddy yelled as the floor shook. The slugs scrunched up their bodies to look as small as possible.

A boy ran in and grabbed a dog bone on the floor. The dog barked and danced around, knocking the shoes over.

The boy tossed the bone out the doorway and raced with his dog to get it.

Squig poked one eye out from under a shoe and looked around. He tapped Buddy with a feeler. "We're fine," he said.

"We have to go home," Buddy said.

"Which way is home?" Squig said looking and feeling. "We might be close. I see some twigs."

Squig slid onto the pretzel sticks. "What's this stuff on the twigs?" he asked.

Buddy saw some loose crystals and yelled, "Salt! You know what the wise old slugs say."

"I know, I know," said Squig, who had fallen on his side and begun to shake. "Salt will dry up your slime. It will dry you up too!"

"Squig, I'll help you," said Buddy.

"You're too little," Squig whispered.

Scott Foresman
Reading

Grade 3
Phonics Reader 22

Earthquakes: What Causes Them?
by Stacey Sparks
illustrated by
Steven Nau

Phonics Skill:
• Consonant /k/ spelled
c, ck, ch

Scott Foresman
Phonics System

Scott Foresman

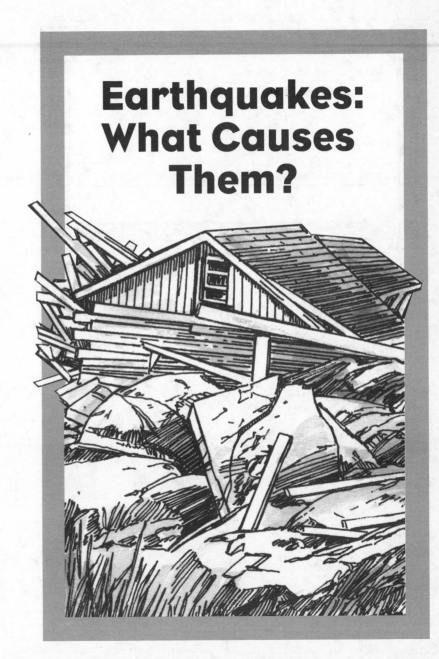

Earthquakes: What Causes Them?

by Stacey Sparks
illustrated by Steven Nau

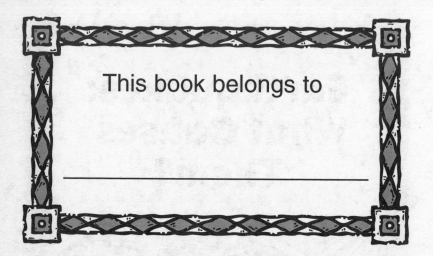

This book belongs to

_____

Phonics for Families: This book provides practice reading words with the *k* sound spelled *c*, *ck*, and *ch*, as in *causes*, *rock*, and *anchors*. Read the book together. Then help your child find the words in this book with the *k* sound spelled *c*, *ck*, and *ch*.

Phonics Skill: Consonant /k/ spelled *c*, *ck*, *ch*

In 1923, a huge wave hit the coast of Japan. An earthquake under the sea caused this wave. Japan has about 1,500 earthquakes every year. Luckily, most of them are small.

Today, we have tools that can tell us when an earthquake is about to happen. These tools give people a chance to leave and find shelter somewhere else—until the Earth is still again.

Earthquakes: What Causes Them?

by Stacey Sparks
illustrated by Stephen Nau

Scott Foresman

Editorial Offices: Glenview, Illinois • New York, New York
Sales Offices: Reading, Massachusetts • Duluth, Georgia
Glenview, Illinois • Carrollton, Texas • Menlo Park, California

Before

After

Think about the ground under your feet. It is solid. It is safe. It is still. The ground is all of these things—most of the time.

But sometimes, in some places, the ground shakes. This is called an earthquake.

Other areas have also been hit with strong earthquakes. In 1964, a big quake hit Alaska. The ground shook for nearly seven minutes. Cars bounced up and down. Houses split in two; streets opened up. When the quake was over, much of Alaska's coast had a new shape.

The flames moved quickly. The city burned for days! When the blaze ended, about 490 city blocks had burned down. More than 200,000 people were homeless.

Once every thirty seconds there is a little earthquake somewhere in the world. People may feel the earth move, but nothing serious happens.

Every few months, there is a major quake somewhere. Cracks open in the ground. Buildings and bridges fall down.

Some earthquakes cause huge waves. When these waves hit harbors, they can pull boats off their anchors and toss them onto the land.

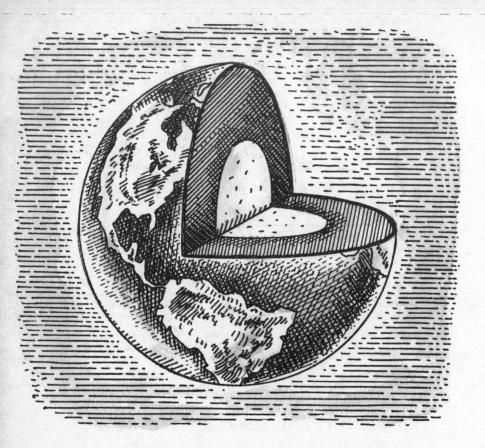

To understand earthquakes, it helps to know more about the Earth.

The Earth is made of three layers of rock. The top layer is the crust. It is between five and thirty miles thick. The next layer is the mantle. It is almost two thousand miles thick. The center of the Earth is called the core. It is over two thousand miles thick.

Under the city streets, there were pipes. Some carried water, while others carried gas for lighting stoves and lamps.

The earthquake cracked many of the gas pipes. Gas leaked into the streets. Fires broke out.

Firefighters sped to put out the flames. They turned on the hydrants and waited, but no water gushed out.

The water pipes had cracked too.

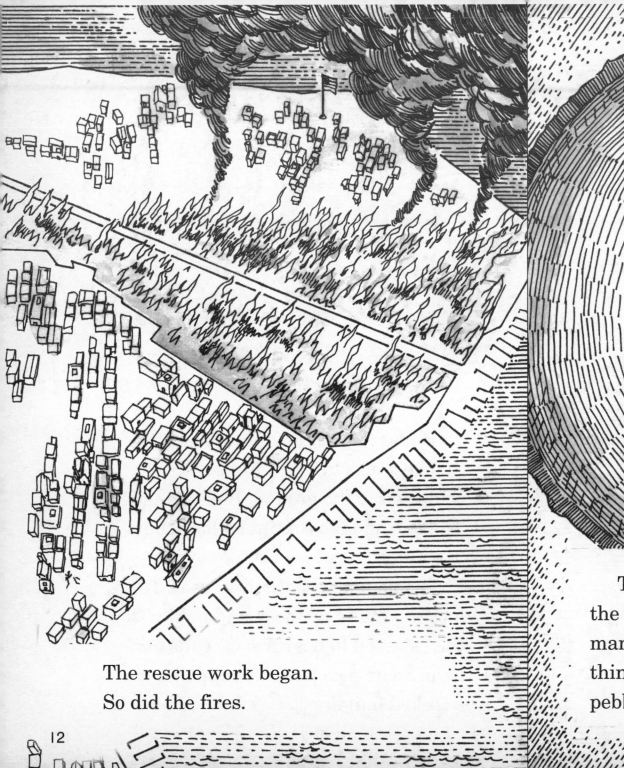

The rescue work began.
So did the fires.

Crust

Mantle

Core

The core of the Earth is very hot. So is the mantle. Some of the rock in the mantle is so hot that it has melted. Just think of it! This rock is not hard like a pebble. It is soft, like paste.

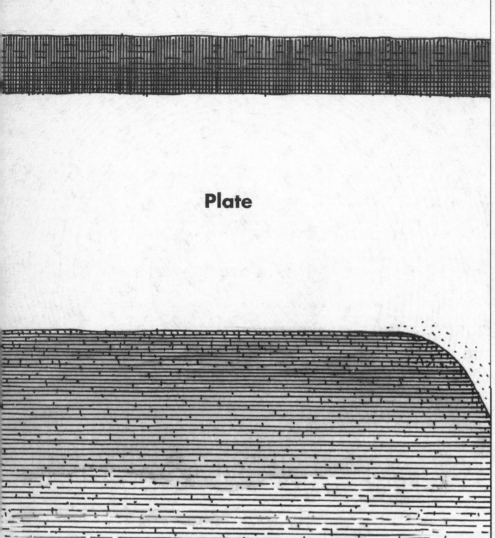

Plate

The hot rock in the Earth's mantle is moving. It flows and bubbles, like boiling water in a pan.

The moving rock of the mantle pushes against the crust.

Houses began to vibrate and sway. Smokestacks toppled. Big buildings collapsed to the ground. Bells clanged. The earthquake continued for about one minute.

People fled from their houses. They looked around in shock and panic. Then they started to hear frantic calls for help. Some people were trapped under wrecked buildings.

It was the morning of April 18, 1906, and most people were still in bed.

A man awakened early to a scene that shocked him. The street was moving in waves. It looked as if the land had become the sea.

Fault

Plate

The Earth's crust is not one solid piece of rock. It is made up of many pieces, or plates. These plates fit together like parts of a puzzle.

The place where two parts of the crust meet is called a fault.

The Earth's Fault Lines

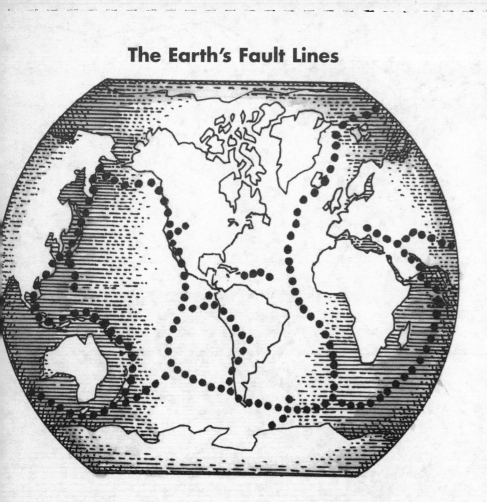

When melted rock pushes up against the plates, they move. Sometimes they slide smoothly, and no one feels anything. At other times, they bump hard against each other. Then the Earth shakes.

Most earthquakes happen along the Earth's fault lines.

8

San Francisco is one of the most beautiful cities in the world. But it is built over a fault. In 1906, the Earth shook along this fault. The earthquake almost destroyed this city.

9

Scott Foresman
Reading

Grade 3
Phonics Reader 23

**The Case of the
Impolite Poodle**
by Lucy Floyd
illustrated by
Randy Chewning

Phonics Skill:
• Prefixes *im-*, *dis-*, *non-*

Scott Foresman
**Phonics
System**

Scott Foresman

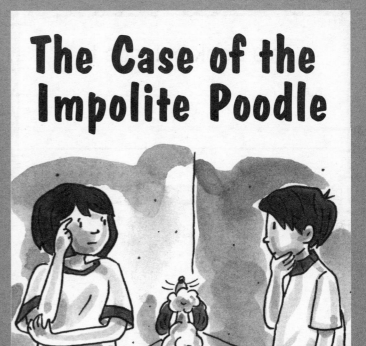

The Case of the
Impolite Poodle

by Lucy Floyd
illustrated by Randy Chewning

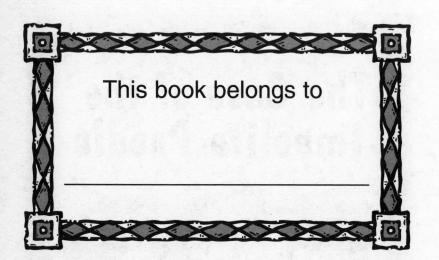

This book belongs to

_____

Phonics for Families: This book features words that begin with *im-*, *dis-*, and *non-*, as in *impolite*, *disappear*, and *nonstop*. Read the book with your child. Then ask him or her to point out and read the words that begin with *im-*, *dis-*, and *non-*.

Phonics Skill: Prefixes *im-*, *dis-*, *non-*

"The Case of the Impolite Poodle is solved!" I say to Carlos.

The girl takes her poodle. I take Poco.

"I'm going to get you a name tag!" I tell Poco. "I don't want this to happen again!"

The Case of the Impolite Poodle

by Lucy Floyd
illustrated by Randy Chewning

Scott Foresman

Editorial Offices: Glenview, Illinois • New York, New York
Sales Offices: Reading, Massachusetts • Duluth, Georgia
Glenview, Illinois • Carrollton, Texas • Menlo Park, California

It is Saturday morning. I am in the park with Poco, my toy poodle. "Do you want to run on the grass, Poco?" I ask. Poco wiggles happily and runs off. My Poco is always happy. I watch her disappear behind a tree.

"I think I have your poodle!" I tell the girl as I point to the dog under the slide. "And you have mine! Our poodles look exactly the same, and we got them mixed up!"

The girl begins to smile. "So that's why she's acting so strangely!" she says. "I saw her by the tree, and I picked her up. I thought she was my poodle!"

A girl comes into the park. She has a poodle on a leash. It is a little toy poodle. I run to the girl. The poodle begins to pull on the leash.

I hear a voice yell, "Hi, Carmen!" I look around and see Carlos. He is my best friend. Sometimes Carlos and I disagree, but we are still friends.

"Where's Poco?" Carlos asks.

"She's running around, the way she always does," I answer. "You know Poco. She's always moving. You could call her a nonstop poodle."

© Scott Foresman 3

There are now many people in the park. There are also many dogs. Carlos and I swing for a few minutes. Then we decide to go to my house for a snack.

"Come on, Poco," I yell.

We wait, but Poco doesn't come. I yell for her again. No Poco!

"That's funny," I say. "Poco always comes when I call her."

We sit in the park a long time. Carlos begins to get impatient.

"It's no use," he says.

I, however, do not give up. I look at the sad little poodle under the slide. I think I know why she is sad.

"It's time for supper," Carlos says.

I know that. I know Mom wants to leave now. But I have to wait!

Then I see something. "We may be able to solve this case," I say.

I look around the park. There are many people and dogs. I have an idea. I tell my idea to Carlos.

"Maybe," he says.

"Maybe she ran away," Carlos says.

"That's impossible," I say. "She never runs away. We come here every day, and she comes when I call her."

"I'll help you look," Carlos says.

We look behind the tree and around the bars. We even look in the can where people throw trash. No Poco!

"Maybe someone stole her," Carlos says.

"That's nonsense!" I say. "Who would be so dishonest?"

Then Carlos looks under the slide.
"I see one toy poodle!" he yells.
"Poco!" I shout. "Why were you hiding?"
I am so glad to see her. But what is wrong with her? She is not happy.
"Did a big dog scare you?" I ask. "Never mind. You'll be all right."

"Let's take her back to the park," I say. "Maybe she's just mad because we brought her home."
But when we get to the park, she runs over to the slide and hides under it again. She just sits there like an immovable statue. She isn't happy in the park either.

We take the sad poodle back to my house. She will have nothing to do with me. I am beginning to get impatient.

"Not only is she sitting in the corner," I say, "but she has her back turned to us. Now that's impolite! Why is she acting so impossible?"

"It's a mystery," Carlos says. "You could call it 'The Case of the Impolite Poodle.'"

"Well, it's a case we have to solve," I say.

But she is not all right. When we get to my house, I try to get her to eat. She will not eat. I try to pick her up. She runs from me. I call her. She will not come. I try scolding her. "You are being impossible, Poco!" I say. She just sits in the corner.

I don't know what to do. I pull out a nonfiction book about dogs. I try to find out why a happy little dog is suddenly so sad. But I cannot find the answer.

"Let's take her to the vet," Carlos says. "Maybe he can discover what's wrong with her."

"That's a good idea," I say. "Let's do it!"

The vet checks my poodle very carefully. He asks me some questions. Then he says, "There doesn't seem to be anything wrong with this dog."

I disagree with the vet's findings. I am not happy with his answer. I know there is something wrong. I just don't know what it is!

Grade 3
Phonics Reader 24

Polar Bears:
Living in the Arctic
by Susan McCloskey
illustrated by
Eldon Doty

Phonics Skill:
• Inflected endings

Polar Bears: Living in the Arctic

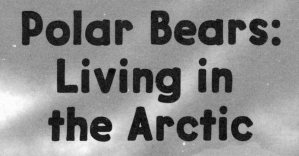

by Susan McCloskey
illustrated by Eldon Doty

This book belongs to

_____

Phonics for Families: This book gives your child practice reading words that have the endings *-ed, -ing, -er,* and *-est*. Read the book with your child. Then have your child go back through the story and make a list of words that have the endings *-ed, -ing, -er,* and *-est*.

Phonics Skill: Inflected endings

The cubs' mother is going to have cubs again. When fall comes, she begins looking for a safe place to dig a warm winter den. In the spring, she will lead her new cubs into the bright, cold air outside the den. Then she will begin teaching them how to live in the harsh but beautiful world of the Arctic.

16

Polar Bears: Living in the Arctic

by Susan McCloskey
illustrated by Eldon Doty

Scott Foresman

Editorial Offices: Glenview, Illinois • New York, New York
Sales Offices: Reading, Massachusetts • Duluth, Georgia
Glenview, Illinois • Carrollton, Texas • Menlo Park, California

What is the biggest meat-eating land
animal in the world? The polar bear!
Male polar bears can weigh more than
a thousand pounds and stand over
eight feet tall.

But the polar bear doesn't start out
big. In fact, newborn polar bear cubs
are smaller than you were when you
were born.

The mother polar bear and her cubs
spend a third winter together. But
when spring comes again, the cubs'
mother, with the help of a male polar
bear, chases the cubs away.

The time has come for the cubs to be
on their own. They have learned all the
skills they need. Now they will begin
taking care of themselves.

© Scott Foresman 3

By the next summer, the cubs are almost as big as their mother. Now they are able to go hunting by themselves, sometimes staying away from her for an hour or more.

Polar bears live in one of the coldest places in the world—the Arctic. This land of snow and ice is so cold that the sea freezes. During much of the winter, the sun never rises. Night lasts twenty-four hours.

How can tiny polar bear cubs live in such a cold, harsh land? They get a lot of help from their moms!

In late fall, a polar bear who is going to have cubs digs a snow cave called a den. Drifting snow soon hides the opening to the den. Snug and warm, the bear sleeps most of the winter. She tries to keep away from the biting winds and fierce storms outside.

The polar bear family stays outside throughout the long, dark winter. They keep warm during storms by curling up together in a big, furry pile.

This is the cubs' first winter outside the warm den where they were born. If they last the winter, they have a good chance of living a long time—perhaps even thirty years.

© Scott Foresman 3

Too soon the Arctic summer is over. The days get colder. The cubs are quite big now, weighing over 130 pounds. But they still have a lot to learn from their mom.

When winter comes and the ocean freezes, the mother polar bear shows her cubs where and how to hunt for food. The cubs watch as their mother waits near a breathing hole in the ice. Sometimes this waiting lasts for hours!

In late December or early January, the cubs are born. Usually there are two. The cubs are about as big as three-week-old kittens. They are blind and covered only with a thin coat of white fur. But their mom's milk is thick and rich. The cubs get bigger and stronger every day. By the time they are two months old, they can move around inside the den. They spend their time chasing each other, digging in the snow, eating, and sleeping.

In February, daylight returns to the Arctic. In March or April, the polar bears leave the den. But not for long! Although the cubs' fur is much thicker and warmer than before, the air is still cold, and the cubs must get used to it. So the family tries to stay close to the den, spending more and more time outside each day.

The cubs have fun climbing, sliding, playing, and sometimes just sitting in the sun with Mom. Meanwhile, they are growing bigger, stronger, and faster.

During the Arctic summer, the cubs keep following their mother, watching her closely. They see her climbing cliffs to look for birds' eggs, diving for seaweed, and chasing geese or ducks. They even see her eating grass.

Now they are big enough to try hunting for themselves. They usually don't catch anything. So it's a good thing they can count on their mom's milk.

© Scott Foresman 3

Besides feeding her cubs and teaching them to hunt, a mother polar bear must also keep them safe. She must even keep them safe from other polar bears.

A male polar bear is much bigger than a female. But a growling female can drive away even the biggest male.

By now Mom is very hungry. It has been almost six months since she has eaten.

At last the cubs are strong enough to follow her as she searches for food. The family leaves the den for good.

Polar bears, like all wild animals, hunt for their food. The mother polar bear sees a seal sleeping on the ice and tries to sneak up on it. The cubs seem to know what is happening. They keep still, watching their mother hunt.

It takes a long time for a polar bear to learn to hunt well. While the cubs are learning, they follow their mom as she looks for food. They keep drinking their mom's milk and getting stronger and stronger. Soon they can walk day and night.

They also can swim, paddling with their front feet and steering with their back feet.

Scott Foresman Reading

Grade 3
Phonics Reader 25

The Whiz Kid and the Whopper
by Sydnie Meltzer Kleinhenz
illustrated by David Austin Clar

Phonics Skills:
- Consonant digraph *wh*
- Consonant /h/ spelled *wh*

Scott Foresman Phonics System

Scott Foresman

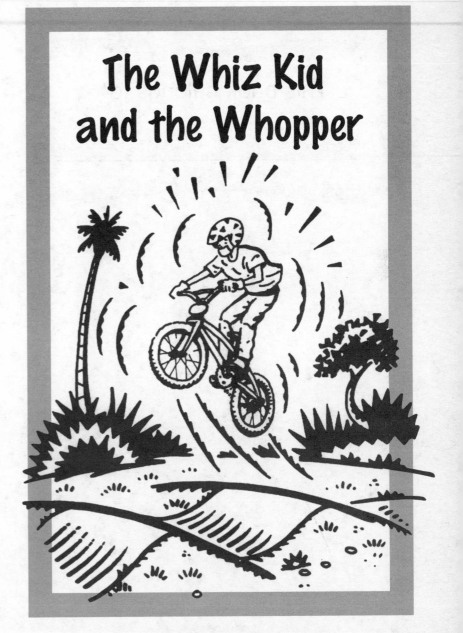

The Whiz Kid and the Whopper

by Sydnie Meltzer Kleinhenz
illustrated by David Austin Clar

This book belongs to

_____

Phonics for Families: This book provides practice reading words that begin with the letters *wh*, such as *what, why,* and *whole.* Enjoy the book with your child. Then have your child read the story to find the words that begin with *wh*.

Phonics Skills: Consonant digraph *wh*; Consonant /h/ spelled *wh*

After the race Ricky joined the crowd around Dan. "Look at that trophy!" Ricky said. "First place! Whew! What a finish!"

"What a bike!" Dan said. "Whenever I made a move, it felt just like my own. Here, this is for you." He handed a State Races sticker to Ricky. "I may be the first-place rider, but this is the first-place bike. And you are a first-place friend!"

The Whiz Kid and the Whopper

by Sydnie Meltzer Kleinhenz
illustrated by David Austin Clar

Scott Foresman

Editorial Offices: Glenview, Illinois • New York, New York
Sales Offices: Reading, Massachusetts • Duluth, Georgia
Glenview, Illinois • Carrollton, Texas • Menlo Park, California

Dan straddled his bike. He put his hands on his hips. "What do you mean you can't ride? We used to go all the time. Whenever you got a chance, you'd go to the practice jumps."

"Whoa!" said Ricky, holding up his hands. "I can't go because I have to walk Whiskers. You know I'm earning money to fix up my bike."

© Scott Foresman 3

Tough break, Ricky thought.

Ricky bent down near Dan. "I'm sorry about your bike," he said kindly. Dan nodded. "Do you want to use mine?" Ricky asked.

Dan looked at Ricky. Then they heard the announcement for the race. "That's a whopper of a favor. Are you sure?" Dan asked.

Ricky nodded and smiled. "Leave the other racers at the starting gate, Whiz Kid!"

Through the bushes, Ricky saw Dan drop his bike on the ground and run to the drinking fountain. The main race must be soon, Ricky thought. Then he went back to scratching the dirt with a stick.

CRUNCH! SCREECH! Ricky looked up.

"Stop! My bike!" Dan yelled as he ran toward a van. The driver stopped and jumped out.

"I'm sorry. I didn't see your bike," the driver said.

Ricky saw Dan drop to his knees and cover his face. He knew Dan was crying.

"Why can't Mrs. Whitney's dog wait until later? The last time I invited you to the jumps, you had to mow her lawn. The time before that, you had to wash her car," Dan said.

"Mrs. Whitney is an old woman who needs help. And I need the money. There will be other people at the practice jumps. You can go show them your speed," Ricky said.

"I think you're avoiding me. Are you mad because I beat you in the State Race?" Dan asked.

"Think whatever you want. But remember, I qualified for the State Races too," Ricky said. "And by the time the races come, I'll have upgraded my bike to be better than yours. And I'll probably beat you easily. So why should I be mad?"

Ricky jogged down the block with Whiskers. Dan did a wheelie and rode the other way.

Everywhere he walked, people patted his shoulder or said, "Tough break." None of it made Ricky feel better. No one could understand how much he wanted to be in the main race. He looked for somewhere to be alone for awhile.

Ricky found a spot somewhat hidden by bushes near the snack bar. He plopped down and tried to hold in a whimper. Ricky stayed hidden. He listened to the announcer calling groups to race.

In the third run, Ricky and Dan raced side-by-side. Once in a while, one would get an edge over the other. Ricky pushed himself into high speed.

When Ricky hit the double jump, he knew his body was too far forward. Ricky's front wheel jammed into the ground. One of his hands whipped off the handlebars. Ricky hit the dirt. His face went white as Dan whizzed to the finish line. Ricky was last.

After walking Whiskers, Ricky rode to the practice jumps. He hid behind a parked car watching and waiting for Dan to leave. "Who does Dan think he is? A whiz kid?" Ricky whispered to himself.

The next day Ricky rode to the bike shop. Jim, the bike shop owner, was standing outside the shop.

"How do you like your new wheels?" Jim asked.

"They're great!" Ricky said. "I've been whizzing up the jumps and whipping around the turns. I plan to win the State Races."

© Scott Foresman 3

Dan was on the inside of the track. Ricky was in the middle.

Ricky took the lead and held it until the second turn. Coming out of the turn, his foot slipped off the pedal. He lost enough speed that Dan and two others passed him. Ricky finished fourth. Dan finished first.

Ricky knew that only eight racers would be in the main race. The third run would be his last chance!

Ricky was able to avoid Dan until the State Races.

Ricky and Dan were at different ends of the starting gate for the first run. Three groups would race three times for one of the eight spots in the main race.

Ricky rode with his mind on the course, not on Dan. He finished second. Dan finished third.

Ricky felt a whole lot better going into the second run.

"It looks as if you and Dan are serious about winning," said Jim. "Dan was in here the other day to put on a better freewheel. When we were done, I watched him whirl around the parking lot for a while."

"That's great," said Ricky feeling as if it wasn't great at all. "I came in to get exactly the same thing."

"Great!" said Jim.

Ricky was practicing when Dan rode up. Dan whistled. Then he yelled, "That's a great double jump, Ricky."

Ricky just nodded at Dan. Then he rode back to the start. His helmet hid his angry face. When Ricky rode the course again, Dan pretended he was a race announcer.

"Whoosh! Ricky's out like a shot. He whisks across the course."

A bubble of laughter filled Ricky's chest. "He's coming to the double jump. He makes it! Whoop-de-doo! Now, Ricky will sign autographs in the tent," Dan yelled.

Ricky held in his laughter. But losing to him wasn't funny. Ricky clenched his teeth. Dan wasn't his friend. Dan was his competition!

© Scott Foresman 3

Scott Foresman
Reading

Grade 3
Phonics Reader 26

**The Story of
Hellen Keller**
by Judy Veramendi
illustrated by
Kay McCabe

Phonics Skill:
• Schwa sound

Scott Foresman
Phonics
System

Scott Foresman

The Story of
Helen Keller

by Judy Veramendi
illustrated by Kay McCabe

This book belongs to

_____

Phonics for Families: This book gives your child practice in reading words that contain an unstressed vowel sound, as in *Helen, teacher,* and *about.* After reading the book together, go back through the story and help your child find and read words that have an unstressed vowel sound.

Phonics Skill: Schwa sound

Helen's life story has been published in many languages. It was the first of several books that she wrote.

Miss Keller traveled around the world with her teacher. She worked hard to help people make better lives for blind and deaf children.

Helen Keller started as a child living in a dark, silent world and went on to become a great woman in American history.

The Story of Helen Keller

by Judy Veramendi
illustrated by Kay McCabe

Scott Foresman

Editorial Offices: Glenview, Illinois • New York, New York
Sales Offices: Reading, Massachusetts • Duluth, Georgia
Glenview, Illinois • Carrollton, Texas • Menlo Park, California

Imagine that you cannot see. Close your eyes and count to sixty. How do you know what is going on around you?

Now continue with your eyes closed. But this time, cover your ears tightly and count to sixty. During these sixty seconds, you will not see and you will not hear.

How do you feel?

Helen learned to read using special books with raised dots. The dots are grouped together to form letters and numbers. Helen also learned to write with a special machine.

Later she went to the Perkins School for the Blind, the same school her teacher had attended. After high school, she went on to college.

While she was in college, she wrote the story of her life.

Then Helen threw herself on the ground and thumped it, asking for its name. Miss Sullivan traced into her hand the letters, g-r-o-u-n-d. After excitedly asking for the names of several more things, Helen touched Miss Sullivan's face, asking for her name. Miss Sullivan spelled t-e-a-c-h-e-r into her hand.

From that day on, no one could stop Helen Keller from learning.

That is the world a little girl named Helen Keller fell into when she was less than two years old. Up to the age of nineteen months, she was a healthy toddler. She loved to explore her home.

But then, she had a sudden illness. She had a high temperature. Nobody quite knows what the illness was. But a few days later, her parents discovered that Helen was losing both her eyesight and hearing.

How did they know this?

Helen did not blink. And she did not react to a strong light or clapping in front of her face.

Soon Helen's world was limited to that empty, silent black space you felt for sixty seconds at the beginning of this story.

And she was not even two years old!

No one could help her understand how or why this had happened.

After one difficult day working with Helen, Miss Sullivan decided to take her for a walk. As they paused for a drink at the outdoor pump, something happened!

Miss Sullivan pumped some water. Helen let the water run into her hand. At the same time, Miss Sullivan spelled w-a-t-e-r into her other hand. Helen excitedly spelled back, asking her teacher for more water. Miss Sullivan pumped out some more water. Helen spelled *water* again.

However, Miss Sullivan was worried. She felt that Helen was not making the connection between the spelling and the thing itself. Helen could copy what Miss Sullivan spelled, but she never spelled a word into Miss Sullivan's hand to ask for something.

Miss Sullivan knew that Helen was smart. Miss Sullivan was not going to give up!

Helen was healthy, so her body kept growing. And, like all children, she wanted to explore the inside and outside of her family's home. However, in doing this, she had many falls and accidents.

Children learn to speak by listening. Then they copy the words they hear. Since Helen couldn't hear, she didn't learn to speak. She couldn't express feelings and ideas that flooded her mind. Helen grew very angry.

By the age of seven, Helen was out of control. Her parents felt sorry for her. They found it hard to discipline her.

She often refused to bathe or comb her hair. She ran about like a wild animal. She was a danger to her new baby sister.

Helen's parents did not know what to do. They wrote to a famous school for the blind in hope of getting some help.

Annie Sullivan, a student who went to this school, agreed to work with Helen. Annie was once blind. But she could now see after several operations.

Once Helen learned how to behave, Miss Sullivan began to teach her how to communicate with others.

She began by trying to help Helen connect things with their names. Miss Sullivan did this by tracing the letters of a word in Helen's hand. Then she had Helen feel the thing she just spelled. For example, Miss Sullivan would trace the spelling for *doll*, d-o-l-l, into Helen's hand. Then she would lead Helen's other hand to touch her doll. Helen quickly copied all the spellings Miss Sullivan traced.

© Scott Foresman 3

Miss Sullivan asked Helen's parents if she and Helen could move into the cottage. She told them that it would be better to work in a new setting. Helen's parents agreed, and the experiment began.

During the first few days, there were several big battles with Helen. But the little girl soon showed how smart she was. She began eating off her own plate with a fork and spoon. She even learned to knit!

Miss Sullivan took a train to the town where Helen lived. She arrived on March 3, 1887.

Years later, Helen said that the date Annie arrived was more important to her than the date she was born. She said it was the beginning of a new life for her.

Miss Sullivan was greeted by a wild, dirty little girl. Helen pushed Miss Sullivan away. She broke two of her teacher's teeth and a lovely doll Miss Sullivan had given her.

© Scott Foresman 3

Miss Sullivan was shocked by the way Helen was allowed to act. As the family tried to talk at dinner, Helen ran from plate to plate, stuffing food in her mouth with her fingers.

When Helen paused by Miss Sullivan's plate and tried to eat off it, Miss Sullivan slapped her hand.

Helen smacked Miss Sullivan back.

The battle for Helen's new life had begun.

Miss Sullivan realized that she was faced with a difficult job. She had to teach Helen sign language. But more importantly, she had to help bring out the wonderful parts of Helen. These things were hidden deep inside an angry, wild child.

Miss Sullivan knew that this job would be impossible in Helen's home. Helen had run wild there for too long. Miss Sullivan needed to find a better place to work. She walked about the grounds of the Keller home. Soon she found a small cottage away from the main house.

Scott Foresman
Reading

Grade 3
Phonics Reader 27

The Brave Little Tailor
retold by Stacey Sparks
illustrated by
Catherine Kanner

Phonics Skill:
• Syllabication and
common syllable
patterns for word
identification

Scott Foresman
Phonics
System

Scott Foresman

The Brave Little Tailor

retold by Stacey Sparks
illustrated by Catherine Kanner

This book belongs to

_____

Phonics for Families: This book provides practice reading words that have two or more syllables, such as *tailor* and *princess*. Some of these words may not be familiar to your child. As you read the book together, help your child figure out the unfamiliar words by finding "chunks" of known words within the longer words. For example, in the word *blackbird* help your child see the words *black* and *bird*; in the word *pretended* help your child see the chunks *pre*, *tend*, and *ed*.

Phonics Skill: Syllabication and common syllable patterns for word identification

NARRATOR: And so the princess married the little tailor. They had a splendid wedding. It was just like a fairy tale!

The Brave Little Tailor

retold by Stacey Sparks
illustrated by Catherine Kanner

Scott Foresman

Editorial Offices: Glenview, Illinois • New York, New York
Sales Offices: Reading, Massachusetts • Duluth, Georgia
Glenview, Illinois • Carrollton, Texas • Menlo Park, California

NARRATOR: Once there was a little tailor. He was very proud of himself.

2

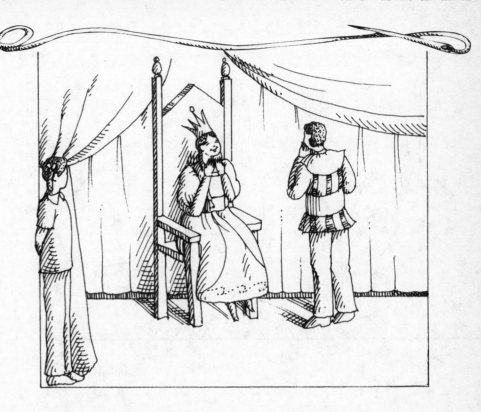

TAILOR: Can you keep a secret?

PRINCESS: Absolutely!

TAILOR: They were not very big monsters.

PRINCESS: No?

TAILOR: In fact, they were quite little.

PRINCESS: How little?

TAILOR: They were about the size of a fly.

PRINCESS: Ha, ha!

TAILOR: In fact, they were flies.

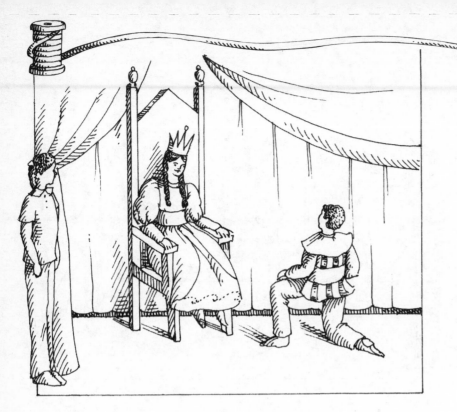

NARRATOR: So the king took the tailor home to meet his daughter.

PRINCESS: Thank you for getting rid of the giant. I am so scared of giants! I am also afraid of toads, barking dogs, and big, strong princes. You are not any of these things. Maybe I will marry you.

TAILOR: I am just a little tailor.

PRINCESS: But what about the seven monsters you got rid of?

TAILOR: I am such a fine tailor! I am such a clever fellow! I am—SO HUNGRY! I have been sewing all day. I need something to eat, but all I have is a dry piece of toast. How boring!

VOICE OUTSIDE: Jam for sale. Good jam!

NARRATOR: The tailor bought some jam for his toast. He ate a few bites. Then he put down the toast and went back to work.

NARRATOR: While the little tailor was sewing, some flies came in the open window. They landed on the sweet, sticky jam.

FLIES: Buzz! Buzz!

NARRATOR: The brave little tailor woke up.

TAILOR: Did someone say my name?

GIANT: Help! I am running away. Far away!

KING AND HELPERS: Look at his belt. "Seven at a throw!" Does that mean seven giants?

TAILOR: No, it means seven buzzing monsters.

KING: Tailor, you have rid my kingdom of a fearsome giant. How can I thank you?

TAILOR: Well, I always thought it would be nice to marry a princess!

NARRATOR: Just then, the king and some of his helpers passed by. When they saw the giant, they froze. For months, this giant had been stomping around the kingdom and scaring everyone.

GIANT: Boo hoo! Don't hurt me!

KING: Are you afraid of us, Giant?

GIANT: I thought little people like you were weak. But if this little tailor is stronger than I am, maybe you are too.

KING: What little tailor?

NARRATOR: When the tailor picked up his toast to finish it, he saw seven flies stuck to the jam.

TAILOR: Yuck! Flies! Well, I must be brave! I will have to get rid of them!

NARRATOR: The tailor threw the toast—and the flies—out the window. Then he was even more proud of himself than before. He wanted the world to know about the amazing thing he had done. So he made a belt to tell the tale.

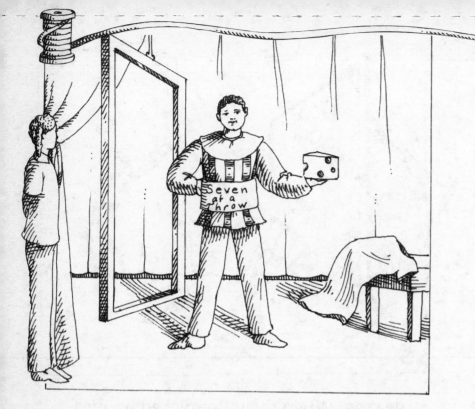

TAILOR: I just got rid of seven monsters with one throw. I was not born to stay at home and be a tailor! Out into the world I must go! I will fight other monsters. Maybe I will marry a princess. But first, I will get a handy chunk of cheese to take on my trip. Just in case I get hungry!

NARRATOR: The tailor set off down the street. People looked at his belt. They were puzzled.

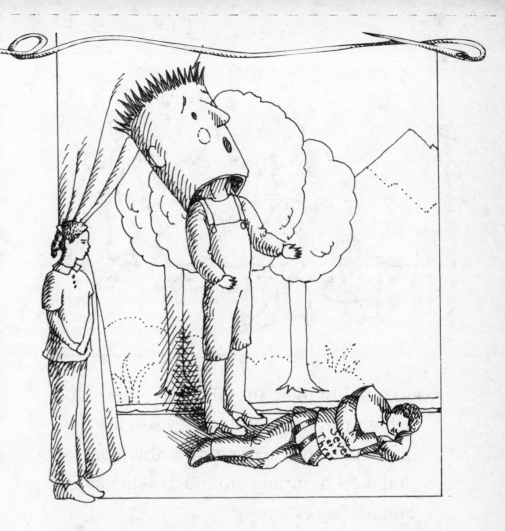

NARRATOR: Time passed. The tailor fell asleep. The giant kept looking up.

GIANT: It has to come down soon! You cannot be that strong, little tailor. No one can throw a rock so high that it never comes down! That's impossible!

© Scott Foresman 3

GIANT: Let's have another contest! You boast that you can throw! So let's have a throwing contest.

NARRATOR: The giant threw a rock way up high. It took a long, long time to come down.

GIANT: Wow!

NARRATOR: Too bad it almost landed on his head.

TAILOR: My turn, big fellow!

NARRATOR: The tailor took the bird out of his sack. He pretended it was a rock and threw it up into the air. The bird flew away.

WOMAN 1: Did you see his belt?

MAN 1: "Seven at a throw!" Sounds scary!

WOMAN 2: But what does it mean?

MAN 2: Who threw? Seven what? Threw where?

TAILOR: I threw seven monsters out the window!

WOMAN 1: Monsters?

TAILOR: Big, hairy, scary, buzzing, horrible monsters with wings!

NARRATOR: The tailor kept walking. Soon he came to the woods. There he found a poor little blackbird. It was stuck in a shrub. The tailor rescued the bird. Then he put it in his sack along with the cheese. He walked a little farther and met a giant.

GIANT: Hi! You're little. I'm big.

TAILOR: I bet you are very smart too.

GIANT: How did you know?

TAILOR: I could just tell. Can you tell that I am very strong?

GIANT: You? Strong? Ha, ha! You make me laugh!

TAILOR: Just look at my belt. "Seven at a throw" means I am strong.

GIANT: Really! Let's see who is stronger.

NARRATOR: So the giant picked up a rock. He squeezed it so hard that water came out. The tailor just smiled and took out his cheese.

TAILOR: I will squeeze milk out of my rock!

NARRATOR: Then he squeezed the cheese until milk came out!

TAILOR: I win!

Scott Foresman
Reading

Grade 3
Phonics Reader 28

**All Because Maud
and Tom Were Bored**
by F. R. Robinson
illustrated by
Albert Lemant

Phonics Skills:
• Vowel digraphs *aw, au*
• /ȯ/ spelled *al*

Scott Foresman
**Phonics
System**

Scott Foresman

All Because
Maud and Tom
Were Bored

by F. R. Robinson
illustrated by Albert Lemant

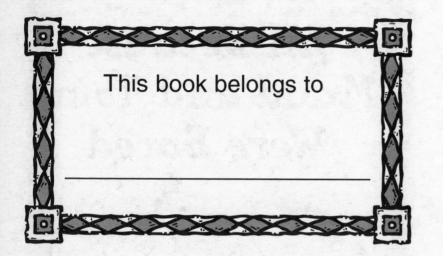

This book belongs to

_____

Phonics for Families: This book features words with the vowel sound heard in *lawn*, *fault*, *call* and spelled *aw*, *au*, and *al*. Read the book together. Then have your child go back through the book and find all the words with the featured vowel sound. You might also have your child name words that rhyme with *saw* and *call*.

Phonics Skills: Vowel digraphs *aw*, *au*; /ȯ/ spelled *al*

Maud and Tom helped their mom
open the first flower shop of the
twenty-third century.

The next thing they knew, people from
all over were buying flowers. Some
people got flowers for themselves. Others
got flowers to give away as gifts.

"People love flowers!" said Tom.

"I'll bet no one ever thought of having
a flower shop before," said Maud.

All Because Maud and Tom Were Bored

by F. R. Robinson
illustrated by Albert Lemant

Scott Foresman

Editorial Offices: Glenview, Illinois • New York, New York
Sales Offices: Reading, Massachusetts • Duluth, Georgia
Glenview, Illinois • Carrollton, Texas • Menlo Park, California

It was August. Maud and Tom were
bored. "This is my least favorite month,"
said Maud.

Tom yawned. "Mine too," he said.
"Summer is almost over and there's
nothing left to do."

"We took our family trip to the moon,"
said Maud.

"We went to space camp," said Tom.

Maud and Tom gathered up the flowers.
"What will we do with them?" asked Tom.

"I know!" said Maud. "Let's give
them away!"

"Yes!" said Tom. "I'll bet people
would love these things!"

Maud and Tom tied the flowers into
bunches. Then they went out and gave
flowers to everyone they saw. People
were thrilled.

"I think we've started something,"
said Maud.

"This must be Rover's fault," said Maud. "He crashed into the machine and changed the settings."

"I don't think this is Rover's fault," said Mom sternly. "You should have asked if you could use the Plant-O-Matic."

"I know," said Maud.

"We're sorry," said Tom.

"Now you're going to have to clean this up. And you'll have to think of something to do with all these flowers," said Mom.

"I've drawn all the computer pictures I can," Maud cried as she looked at the artwork on the wall.

"And I'm tired of talking to my robot," said Tom. The robot squawked. "Sorry," said Tom.

"So now what can we do?" asked Maud.

There was a clicking sound from the den. Tom and Maud looked at each other.

"The Plant-O-Matic is not being used," said Maud. "Are you thinking what I'm thinking?"

Tom paused for a second. "Maybe," he said.

Then Tom and Maud dashed down the hall to the den.

4

Maud and Tom's mom walked in. "Help!" called Maud and Tom.

Mom pushed some buttons. Soon the flowers stopped coming out of the Plant-O-Matic.

Maud filled another glass and then another. "These are pretty, but I think we have all we need," she said.

"I think we have a problem!" said Tom.

Large flowers were filling up the room. They were spilling into the hall.

"You set the number dial at *ten*, right?" asked Maud.

"Yes, but that's not what it says now!" said Tom. "It says ten thousand!"

"This is awful!" said Maud.

They studied the Plant-O-Matic. It had lots of knobs and switches. There was a list of plants on the front.

"Grass," read Tom.

"For the lawn," snickered Maud. She pointed to the patch of grass in the pot.

"Trees," said Tom.

"For shade," said Maud, pointing to the shadow by the tree in the corner.

"Vegetables," said Tom.

"For dinner!" they both giggled.

Tom and Maud looked at the pictures of plants their mom had hung on the walls. "Too bad plants don't grow by themselves anymore," said Maud sadly.

"Mom said that by the year 2200 there were no more forests, farms, or lawns. That's because there was no space for them," Tom said.

"It's a good thing she invented the Plant-O-Matic. At least we have plants here," said Maud.

"Press the GO button," read Maud. Tom did. The Plant-O-Matic started to hum.

Soon a big flower came out. Maud and Tom applauded. Then out came another one. "They smell so nice!" said Maud, holding a flower to her nose.

"Where should we put them?" Tom asked.

Maud grabbed a glass. She filled it full of flowers.

Just then Rover ran in. "Stop, Rover!"
called Maud. Rover ran around and
around the room. It seemed he had
crashed into everything before Maud
could stop him.

"What a crazy pet!" said Tom. He
turned back to the Plant-O-Matic. "Now
where were we?"

Tom went back to the list of plants.
"Flowers," he said. "What are flowers?"

"I don't know. Let's look in this book,"
said Maud, reaching for a book called
Flowers of Long Ago.

She opened the book. They both
looked at the pictures. "What do you think
flowers were for?"

"Who knows? But they're awfully
pretty," said Tom.

There was another long pause.
"Are you thinking what I'm thinking?"
said Tom.

"Maybe," said Maud.

"Do you think Mom will mind?"
asked Tom.

"Well, she let me help her use the
Plant-O-Matic once," said Maud.

"She'll like flowers. We'll give them
to her!" said Tom.

Maud found the Plant-O-Matic
instruction book. She read, "Pick the
kind of plant you want."

Tom pushed the flowers button.

"Pick the size plant you want,"
Maud read.

Tom turned the knob to *small*.

Maud read on. "Set the number switch
to the number of plants you want."

Tom set the switch at *ten*.

Scott Foresman
Reading

Grade 3
Phonics Reader 29

Inventions, Old and New
by Anastasia Suen
illustrated by
Chris Celusniak

Phonics Skill:
• Vowel digraphs *ui, ew*

Scott Foresman
Phonics System

Scott Foresman

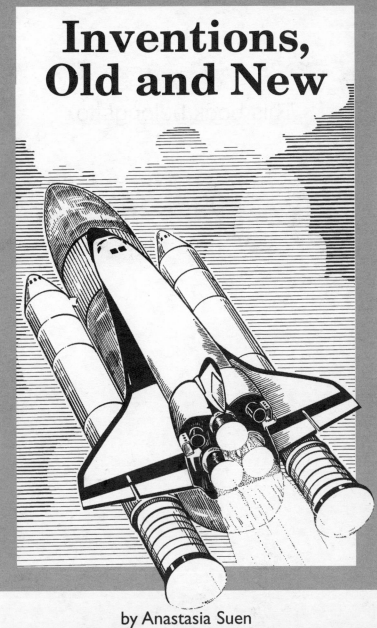

Inventions, Old and New

by Anastasia Suen
illustrated by Chris Celusniak

This book belongs to

_____

Phonics for Families: This book provides practice reading words that contain the vowel sound heard in *fruits* and *new*. Read the book together. Then as you reread the book, have your child point out the words that have the same vowel sound as *fruits* and *new*.

Phonics Skill: Vowel digraphs *ui, ew*

Maiman

Edison

Zworykin

Marconi

Bell

Hopper

There are many people who invented the things we have today. Although these people came from different parts of the world, they all had one thing in common. They were all hard workers. They didn't give up. When something didn't work, they tried again. Knowing what didn't work helped them find out what did work!

Inventions, Old and New

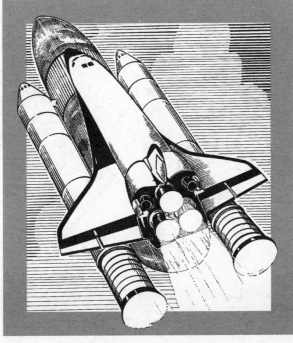

by Anastasia Suen
illustrated by Chris Celusniak

Scott Foresman

Editorial Offices: Glenview, Illinois • New York, New York
Sales Offices: Reading, Massachusetts • Duluth, Georgia
Glenview, Illinois • Carrollton, Texas • Menlo Park, California

What is an invention?

An invention is something new. However, only a few inventions are completely new. Most of the time, inventors use something that has already been invented when they make their new inventions.

Inventions change the way people live. Most inventions help people live better, easier lives.

Let's look at a few of these inventions!

2

Some inventions have led us far and wide! Alice Chatham invented a new kind of mask for pilots to wear when they flew in jets high above the clouds. She made helmets too. When the first pilot flew faster than sound, he was wearing a helmet that Chatham had invented. Years later, Chatham made space suits and helmets for the astronauts.

15

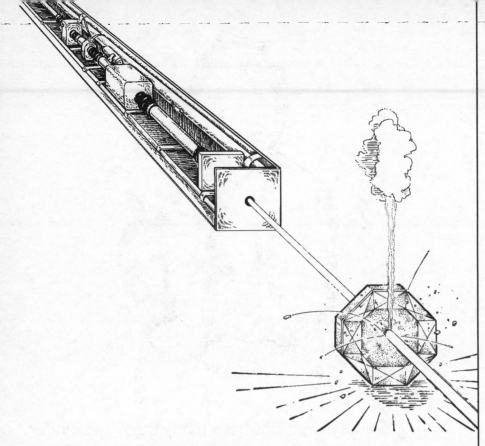

Another invention that has many uses is the laser. Theodore Maiman built the first working laser. A laser is a very bright, hot light. The beam of light travels in a straight line. It is very powerful. It can drill a hole in a diamond, read and play back music on a compact disc (CD), and sort mail. Doctors also use lasers in operations. This is another invention that has greatly changed people's lives.

Thomas Edison is one of our country's most famous inventors. He worked on more than a thousand inventions. He invented the first machine to make moving pictures. He invented the phonograph, which was the first machine to record sounds and play them back. He also worked on other people's inventions and made them better.

Some inventions come as a surprise. When Levi Strauss heard that gold had been discovered, he went to seek his fortune. He didn't dig for gold. He sold cloth to make tents.

As the miners panned for gold, they ruined their clothes. A miner told Strauss he should make pants, instead of selling cloth for tents.

Strauss made blue pants. He hammered rivets to the pockets so they wouldn't tear. The miners loved their new blue jeans!

Some inventions have many uses. Alexander Parkes first invented plastic. So many of the things we use today are made of plastic! This teddy bear is made of plastic both inside and out. The bear's soft fur is really plastic that has been shot through tiny holes. The pieces that come through the holes are used to form the bear's fur. The inside of the bear is stuffed with another kind of plastic. Even the bear's eyes are made of plastic!

Some inventions are made by accident. Charles Goodyear accidentally dropped some natural rubber and sulfur onto a hot stove. A new kind of rubber was invented!

This new rubber did not break easily in the cold or get sticky in the heat. This new rubber is used in tires, raincoats, and other waterproof things. What a good accident!

Levi Strauss would not have been able to make jeans without the invention that Harriet Slater had made years earlier. Long before Levi Strauss was born, Harriet Slater found a new way to make thread. She was given a patent for her invention. This meant that no one else could use her idea without asking her. A patent lasts for seventeen years. She was the first woman in the United States to hold a patent.

Some people invent to make money. Some invent because they enjoy trying out new ideas. And others invent because they see something is needed.

Harriet W. R. Strong was a farmer. Her crops needed to be watered. She could not count on the rain to water her crops properly. Her needs led her to invent a way to water her crops when there wasn't enough rain. Her invention gave the crops just the right amount of water and made it possible to grow more fruits and vegetables.

© Scott Foresman 3

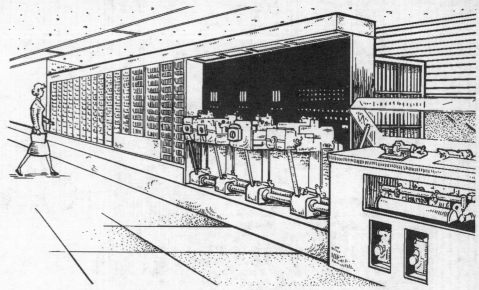

Sometimes inventions need to be made easier to use before people will buy them. This is what happened with computers. When computers were first invented, they were very large. Some were more than forty-eight feet long. They were also very difficult to use. Only a few people knew how to use them because everything had to be written in code.

Grace Murray Hopper invented a computer language that made it easier for people to work with computers. And other people invented other things that helped make the computers what they are today.

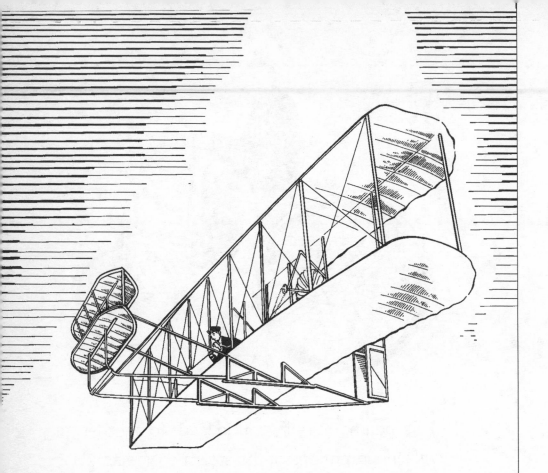

An invention can fulfill the greatest dream! For hundreds of years, people had dreamed of flying. Orville and Wilbur Wright were brothers who dreamed of flying too. They invented the first airplane. They tried out their ideas over and over with kites and gliders, with motors and wires. Then one day they flew!

Sometimes one invention causes the need for other inventions. Once the farmers had more crops, they were able to sell them to the people in the city. But, there was one problem—how would they get the crops to the city without having them go bad. If the food was too hot when it was shipped, it would spoil. If the food was too cold, it would dry out and taste bad.

Mary Pennington studied ways to keep the food fresh on its way from the farm to the city. She invented a way to cool food so it would taste good and not spoil.

Some inventions change over time. The first bicycles were built over 200 years ago. They were made of wood and had no pedals or steering bar. Kirkpatrick MacMillan changed the bicycle. His invention had pedals and handlebars for steering. Over the years, other inventors added chains, spokes, and inflatable tires.

Sometimes one invention leads to another. With the inventions of the steam engine and then the gasoline engine, came the invention of the automobile. Gottlieb Daimler and Karl Benz built the first automobile in 1885. This invention greatly changed people's lives!

As more and more cars were made, the need for other things, such as steel, rubber, and glass grew and grew. New jobs opened up and people moved to new homes outside the big cities.

© Scott Foresman 3

Scott Foresman
Reading

Grade 3
Phonics Reader 30

**Penny's Unusually
Good Day**
by Susan Blackaby
illustrated by
Stephanie O'Shaughnessy

Phonics Skill:
• Affixes

Scott Foresman
Phonics
System

Scott Foresman

Penny's Unusually Good Day

by Susan Blackaby
illustrated by Stephanie O'Shaughnessy

This book belongs to

_____

Phonics for Families: This book gives your child an opportunity to read words that have more than one affix, such as *unseasonably* and *impatiently*. As you read the book with your child, help him or her identify root words and spot the prefixes and suffixes that have been added.

Phonics Skill: Affixes

Back at the bakery, the smell of fresh-baked rolls was unmistakable.

"I am simply starving," said Penny. "Let's have a picnic!" Penny got out the apples and cheese while Manny put two rolls on a plate.

"This is undoubtedly the best picnic I have ever been on," said Penny happily. "I could stay right here forever."

"What would Lucky say about that?" asked Manny.

"Woof, woof, woof," said Penny.

16

Penny's Unusually Good Day

by Susan Blackaby
illustrated by Stephanie O'Shaughnessy

Scott Foresman

Editorial Offices: Glenview, Illinois • New York, New York
Sales Offices: Reading, Massachusetts • Duluth, Georgia
Glenview, Illinois • Carrollton, Texas • Menlo Park, California

It was shopping day. Penny got her list and her basket. She headed for High Street with her dog, Lucky. The day was sunny and unseasonably warm. Lucky walked ahead of Penny, sniffing his way up the street. He seemed to be on the trail of a discovery.

The pet shop was the only store Lucky could enter. He sniffed his way all around the store and got a treat from the owner.

"This old dog of yours is pretty well used," said the owner, scratching Lucky's ears. "I'd say he is nonreturnable!"

"I guess I will keep him, then," joked Penny.

2

© Scott Foresman 3

15

Penny stopped next at the drug store to get a new pen.

"This one writes in purple," said the lady behind the counter. "And it is refillable, when it runs dry."

"That will be handy," said Penny.

Now and then Lucky would stop in his tracks and stand immovable, with a far-off look in his eye. Penny tugged on his leash impatiently.

"Come on! Keep moving, you silly dog," she said, pulling and pleading.

The first shop they came to was the bakery. Penny tied Lucky to a seat near the door.

"Down," said Penny, pointing at the ground. Lucky folded his legs and plopped down. "Stay!" said Penny, putting her hand in front of Lucky's wet, black nose. Lucky put his chin on his paws.

Penny and Lucky went up the street to the fruit stand. Lucky stayed by a bench while Penny shopped.

Penny got apples, pears, and bananas. She dropped two lemons on the floor. They bounced and rolled under a box. "It is a good thing they are unbreakable," said Penny, bending down to pick them up.

© Scott Foresman 3

At the cheese shop, Penny tied Lucky to a tree. She went in and got two large pieces of very smelly cheese.

"This is very cheesy," said the cheese man as he wrapped up her order.

"Well, you would not want uncheesy cheese!" laughed Penny.

Penny walked into the bakery. "Oh, what an unbelievable smell!" she said, smiling at the man behind the counter.

"Good morning," said the man. He was wearing a remarkably tall white hat that bobbed when he tipped his head. "My name is Manny. May I help you?"

"Well," said Penny, "I don't know where to start. Everything looks unusually good."

"I know the feeling," Manny nodded. "It can be impossibly hard to choose," he said. "Even I have a hard time, and I baked it all myself!"

"Lucky! That is disgraceful!" scolded Penny. To Jean she said, "Tea would be so nice. I have been hopelessly busy lately, but I will call you next week."

"All right," said Jean cheerfully. "I look forward to seeing you soon."

Penny snapped Lucky's leash and they went on their way.

Penny stepped out of the shop. Lucky jumped up. He danced impatiently when he saw her come through the door.

"Lucky," said Penny. "Our next stop is the cheese shop."

On their way down the street, they met their neighbor, Jean.

"Penny! We must get together for tea. I hardly ever get to see you anymore," said Jean.

Lucky licked the toe of Jean's shoe.

"I need some muffins for breakfast, some bread for lunch, and some rolls for dinner," said Penny.

Manny tapped his head thoughtfully.

BAKERY

"The poppy seed muffins are uncommonly tasty," said Manny. "And this brown bread is good with soup."

"That will be fine," said Penny. "Now what about rolls? I need a dozen."

"Unfortunately," said Manny, "I don't have any."

"Oh dear," said Penny unhappily.

"But I could make some," said Manny. "You can pick them up on your way home."

"That is a great idea!" said Penny. "I will do the rest of my shopping. Then I will stop back here."

"I will set these things aside for you. See you in a while!" said Manny.